Physical Characteristics of the Japanese Spitz

(from the Fédération Cynologique Internationa̤ ̤reed standard)

Tail: Se̤ ̤n high, moderately long, carried over ba̤ck.

Body: *Withers:* High. *Back:* Straight and short. *Loins:* Broad. *Chest:* Wide and deep, ribs well sprung. *Belly:* Well drawn up.

Hindquarters: Muscular, stifle and hock moderately bent.

Size: *Height at withers:* Dogs 30–38 cm; bitches slightly smaller than dogs.

Feet: Cat feet. Pads thick, and desirably black as well as the nails.

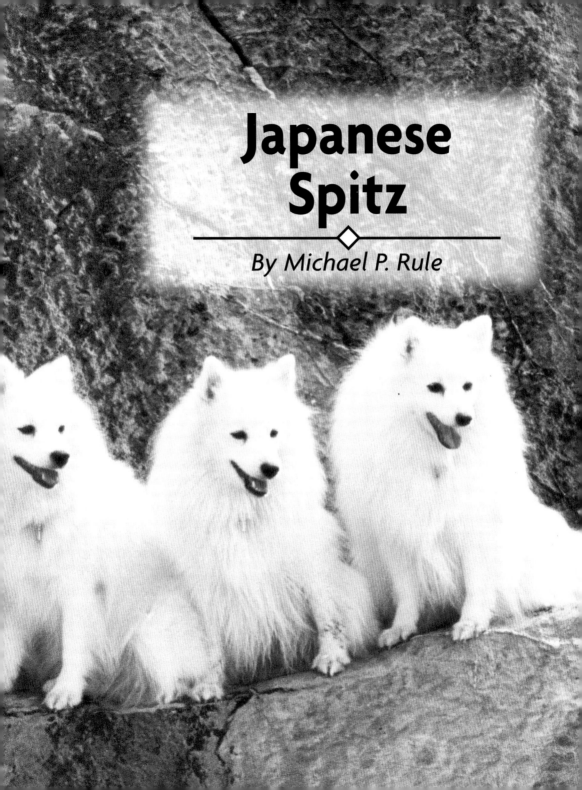

Japanese Spitz

By Michael P. Rule

Contents

KENNEL CLUB BOOKS: JAPANESE SPITZ

ISBN: 1-59378-360-4

Copyright © 2004
Kennel Club Books, Inc., 308 Main Street, Allenhurst, NJ 07711 USA
Cover Design Patented: US 6,435,559 B2 • Printed in South Korea

Photographs by Carol Ann Johnson and Michael P. Rule, with additional photos by:

Malcolm Baird, Norvia Behling, Bernd Brinkmann, T.J. Calhoun, Carolina Biological Supply, Doskocil, Isabelle Francais, James Hayden-Yoav, James R. Hayden, RBP, Bill Jonas, Dwight R. Kuhn, Dr. Dennis Kunkel, Mikki Pet Products, Phototake, Jean Claude Revy, Dr. Andrew Spielman, Alice van Kempen and R. Wilbie.

Illustrations by Patricia Peters, Michael P. Rule and H. R. Spira, BVSc, MRCVS, MACVS, HAD.

The publisher would like to thank all of the owners of the dogs featured in this book, including the Henerasky family, C. Holmstedt, Bill & Pat Moran and Mr. & Mrs. M. P. Rule.

A striking representative of the breed is Eng. Ch. LuSofia Lilac Serenade of Sunset.

HISTORY OF THE

JAPANESE SPITZ

As with the origins of so many intriguing breeds of dog, there is no exact information about the origins of the Japanese Spitz. The breed belongs to the family of Nordic-type spitz dogs represented by many breeds throughout the world. One of the oldest groups of dogs, the spitz breeds share many characteristics, including triangular-shaped heads with small, erect, forward-facing pointed ears, and pointed fox-like muzzles. They have medium or long coats and medium-length tails, carried over their backs. The Japanese Spitz, with its plush, wintry white coat, is often referred to as "like an Arctic fox."

Compared to many other spitz breeds, like the Samoyed or Japanese Shiba Inu, the Japanese Spitz is a relatively new creation, and not a "spinoff" of the larger Samoyed, as some false information might lead people to believe. We know that the Japanese Spitz is reported to have been in Japan as recently as 1920, and the first member of the breed was exhibited at a Tokyo dog show in 1921. Other spitz breed types trace their origins back thousands of years, or make such impressive claims.

Germany is the home of many of the spitz dogs, including the ever-popular Pomeranian as well as the five colorful German Spitz breeds. One excellent theory about the origin of the Japanese Spitz is that the breed descended from white examples of the German Spitz. Several lines of German Spitz were imported into Japan from 1910–1918, via Russia and China. These dogs were referred to as "White Russian Spitz" (a confusing nomenclature that may have been associated with the Samoyed or the Nenets Herding Laika).

Another interesting theory is that the American Eskimo Dog, one of the most popular companion dogs in the US and also a relative of the German Spitz dogs, was brought to Japan on a Canadian rescue cargo ship at the time of the Great Earthquake in Tokyo in 1923. Like the Japanese Spitz, the American Eskimo Dog is solid white and classically spitz in type, and is of a similar size.

Ms. Tomiko Kubota of the Japanese Spitz Association in Japan sent information about the breed's origins to the Japanese Spitz Club of England. Ms. Kubota states, "The history of the Japanese Spitz is relatively short...in the 1930s there was another 'inflow' into Japan of Russian Spitz from Manchuria which

> ## GENUS *CANIS*
> Dogs and wolves are members of the genus *Canis*. Wolves are known scientifically as *Canis lupus* while dogs are known as *Canis domesticus*. Dogs and wolves are known to interbreed. The term "canine" derives from the Latin word *Canis*. The term "dog" has no scientific basis but has been used for thousands of years. The origin of the word "dog" has never been authoritatively ascertained.

The American Eskimo Dog is one of the most popular companion dogs in the US.

could have been due to the Japanese military involvement in the area."

For years, the Japanese called all dogs with long white coats "Samo." This changed in 1935 when the dogs were divided by size, and all larger-type dogs were called "Samo" and the smaller-type dogs were called "Spitz."

Regardless of which theory is correct, we can at least conclude

This group of German Spitz Klein gives an idea of the rainbow of colors seen in this small member of the German Spitz family.

Although the two breeds are members of the spitz family and do resemble each other closely, the Japanese Spitz is not merely an offshoot of the larger Samoyed, shown here, as is often misconceived.

ORIGINAL SPITZ DOGS

One theory that has been stated is that the Japanese Spitz was created from two varieties of dog: the American Eskimo Dog and the White Russian Spitz, possibly a Siberian-laika-type, imported to Japan via Manchuria.

that today's Japanese Spitz was created and developed in Japan by dedicated fanciers between 1920 and 1950.

A great many records were lost or destroyed during or just after World War II. There were many clubs, all of which kept records of

Gainsborough's painting of the actress Mrs. Robinson with her white Pomeranian. The dog in the painting is much larger than the Pomeranian we know today.

dogs and owners. Examples are the Japan Kennel Club (JKC), founded in 1949; the Nippon Spitz Association (NSA), founded in 1959; and others. It has been stated that the Japanese Spitz was very popular with the Japanese Emperor in the late 1950s.

JAPANESE LANGUAGE LESSON

Yuki means "snow."
Hoshi means "star."
Hana means "flower."
Ureshii means "happy."
Akarui means "bright."
Ogamu means "worship."
Kanzen-na means "complete."

The first Japanese Spitz registered by the Japan Kennel Club was Hakuryu-go (White Dragon), sired by Koma-go out of Shinju-go and whelped August 6, 1947. In the *NSA Album* of 1979, there appears a picture of Hakuou-Boy (White King), whelped in 1951. Other early registrations were King of Kinsen, whelped June 28, 1951; Rurshey of Musashiland, whelped February 2, 1953 and Lucky of Shinko-Saw, whelped July 5, 1953.

SPREAD OF THE JAPANESE SPITZ

There are records of a bitch named Sabina of Moonlight living in Norway in 1967, but there is no official import documentation for her. The first import into Europe from Japan came to Sweden in 1973; this dog was Andoleasson of Golden Meadow. Imports into other European countries followed: Norway in 1975; England in 1980; Italy and Denmark in 1985.

In 1976, litter brothers Ch. Hawk of Kagetsuland and Ch. Hover of Kagetsuland, sired by NSA Ch. Floyd Excel of Tokyo Kashusow out of NSA Ch. Animete of Makiesow, arrived in Sweden from Japan. These two dogs proved to be of great influence on the breed in Britain, and either Hawk or Hover appears on most British pedigrees. NSA Ch. Hardery of Kashusow, their litter brother in Japan, whelped November 5, 1975, was a great example of the breed.

Japanese Spitzen being exhibited at a show in the breed's homeland.

Owing to the fact that there was no reciprocal agreement between the English and the Japan Kennel Clubs, the British were unable to import directly from Japan. Records show that the first of the breed to be imported into England came from Sweden. This was a bitch named Alvretens Jicho of Norsken, owned by Mrs. D. Kenyon and registered in November 1977. She was followed soon after by a dog, Alvretens of Namik, owned by Mr. and Mrs. Rodwell and registered in July 1977. He was registered before Jicho, although Jicho was the first to be shown.

The situation changed in 1980 when Miss H. Collins imported the first two dogs directly from Japan. These were the dog Fuji of Oyama Yamamotosow, sired by Abroad of Nakada out of Acacia of Oyama Yoshizawa Kennels, and the bitch Shirayuki of Tokyo Seizansow, sired by Fujimiland 11 Montblanc out of Yuki of Charm Mamy Kennels.

THE BREED IN ENGLAND

The English Kennel Club recognized the Japanese Spitz and registered the first one on July 5, 1977. Registration of the Japanese Spitz Club was passed by the English

No. 1 Hakuryu-go, born in 1947, was the first Japanese Spitz registered with the Japan Kennel Club.

Eng. Ch. Yonala Tiger Lilly at LuSofia was the first British champion.

Kennel Club on January 22, 1981. The club had 40 members, and membership increased to 150 by 1989. The club held its first Open Show within the Southern Counties Championship Show in 1982. The Kennel Club granted championship status to the Japanese Spitz Club in 1988 with 10 sets of Challenge Certificates (CCs); it now has 16 sets per year.

The 1988 Crufts show saw the first set of Challenge Certificates for the breed. The dog winner was Sherivale Osaka of Valdonic, sired by Oldway Prince Charming of Sherivale out of Genza of Sherivale and owned by Mrs. V. Brookes. The bitch winner was Yonala Tiger Lilly at LuSofia, sired by Ridgecross Choshi at Onoyoko out of Oldway Yuki Tama of Helpeton. This bitch, owned by Mrs. V. Stripe, went on to become the breed's first British champion. The breed's first Junior Warrant was won in 1986 by Alkola Yamabuki, sired by Foskars Aki Hinode of Rosedyke out of Astutus Kurakumo of Alkola and owned by Mrs. L. Robson.

JAPANESE BREED NAME
The Japanese Spitz in its country of origin is called the *Nihon Supittsu*, a classic medium-sized spitz. The name translates literally to the English name.

The breed record-holder is Ch. Snowisp of Ice Berg, with 32 CCs, owned by Mrs. J. Coram and sired by Lowerpark Kuniaki out of Allbeam Coco Nut Nice Mattpapp.

THE BREED ON THE CONTINENT
The first Japanese Spitzen were imported from Japan to Finland around the time of the breed's emergence in the UK. The first two Japanese Spitzen in Italy were imported directly from Japan in 1985. One was the bitch Agree of

Shirayuki of Tokyo Seizansow, born February 4, 1983, was the first Japanese Spitz bitch imported to England directly from Japan. She is the grandmother of Eng. Ch. LuSofia Lilac Serenade of Swanset.

Int. Nord. Ch. Hawk of Kagetsu Lana, owned by C. Holmstedt of Sweden, was born May 11, 1975.

Ooka Hiyoshisow, sired by Darling of Usui out of Alice of Senbon Matsubarasow. She unfortunately died at eight months of age. The other was the dog Take-Maru of Yokohama Takada, sired by Alcyon of Port Masuda out of Asa-Giku of Mischief Queen. Following these two was another bitch, Fujiko of White Kodamasow, sired by Twin-kle Jupiter of Lilac Spring out Akane of Wakakusa Land.

By 1986, the breed also was represented in Austria, Germany, Holland and Switzerland. Today, the breed in each of these countries enjoys a small but loyal following.

JAPANESE SPITZEN TODAY
Australia imported its first two Japanese Spitzen from England in 1980: a dog, Norsken Amida, sired by Alvretens Omonzuru of Norsken out of Alvretens Jicho of Norsken; and a bitch, Norsken Daibutsu, sired by Alvretens Omonzuru of Norsken out of Alvretens Richiigi of Norsken.

There are no AKC-registered Japanese Spitzen in America, as the breed is not recognized by the American Kennel Club. The breed

---

BREED CLUB IN THE UK
Mrs. Margo Emerson of the UK conceived the idea of forming Britain's Japanese Spitz Club. The founding members had an inaugural meeting in the YMCA off the Tottenham Court Road in London on August 3, 1980. In attendance were 27 people, 12 of whom owned Japanese Spitzen.

Yonala Tiger Lilly at LuSofia (bitch) and Sherivale Osaka of Valdonic (dog) were the first two Challenge Certificate winners in England.

A SHINING RARE-BREED SHOW DOG
To show how well the breed was doing in the UK during the early 1980s, a Japanese Spitz won the Any Variety Not Separately Classified Utility at the Crufts Dog Show in 1982, 1983 and 1984.

is recognized by the American Rare Breed Association (ARBA), the Continental Kennel Club (CKC) and the National Kennel Club (NKC), all of which are smaller American registries dedicated to rare breeds, as well as by the Canadian Kennel Club.

At the height of the breed's popularity in Japan in 1958, 4,912 Japanese Spitzen were registered. This figure dropped to 356 in 1976, which was an all-time low. The breed then started to make a comeback and, by 1994, registrations were up to 1,803. Registration numbers continue to rise and, at the present time, the Japanese Spitz is in the top 20 most popular breeds in Japan.

Eng. Ch. Alkola Yamabuki, the UK's first Junior Warrant winner.

A modern
Japanese Spitz,
illustrating the
breed's beautiful
abundant white
coat.

The alert, lively, happy nature that makes the Japanese Spitz a wonderful companion is evident just by looking at him.

JAPANESE SPITZ

LOOKS AND PERSONALITY

The Japanese Spitz makes a delightful pet dog for his many positive attributes. He is an alert, intelligent, lively, happy, medium-sized dog who always is happy to be with people, including children of most ages, and other animals. Very affectionate and a real companion, the dog is slightly chary upon first meeting strangers.

The Japanese Spitz has a pure white double coat (meaning a harsher longer outer coat and a plush thicker undercoat), contrasted by his excellent black pigment on the eyerims, nose pad, lips, nails and footpads. His dark expressive eyes will worm their way into any dog lover's heart. The eye shape is described as that of a Gingko nut, an ancient Chinese nut. The ears are small, triangular in shape, erect and facing forward. The tail is of moderate length, profusely coated with long hair and carried over the center of the back, never hanging down to the side. The teeth should be strong, with jaws close and a regular scissors bite.

A Japanese Spitz should be considered an adult at 12 months or older, although some mature much earlier than others. Bitches can have their first season as young as six months old, but they should not be bred from until they are fully mature. Dogs to be used at stud, likewise, need to know what a bitch in season is "all about" and should not breed until around 12 months of age.

FROM THE GERMAN, *SPITZ*...

The name of the breed originates from *spitz*, a German word meaning "something pointed," referring to the breed's pointed muzzle that forms a wedge shape.

Japanese Spitz is a pack of several of these snow-white beauties, stepping out in the sun with their glistening white coats, the silver tips of their hair shining as a gentle breeze blows through the coats to highlight this shimmering effect.

The Japanese Spitz breed was used at its peak in Japan as a watchdog. Though he should never be considered a noisy dog, he has a loud bark that he uses to let you know when someone is about or something is going on. The Japanese Spitz does not tend to be a biter nor is he aggressive toward people or other animals. Nevertheless, he keeps a careful watch on his home, using his voice with discretion, a trait not found in some other "barky" spitz breeds.

Always prepared to join in with the family activities, the Japanese Spitz makes a handsome addition to the "family portrait." Owners find that the only thing that looks more lovely than a

Today, the Japanese Spitz is mainly a companion dog, appealing because of his affectionate nature and striking appearance. Japanese Spitzen are very sensitive dogs who respond well to training if approached with love and kindness. They will not appreciate or accept harsh treatment, either physical or verbal. The breed is also prized for its sense of humor, a trait that leads owners to share many delightful anecdotes about their Japanese Spitzen's near-human responses to situations or ingenious solutions to puzzling problems.

HELP WANTED: THERAPY DOG

Many owners take advantage of their Japanese Spitzen's affinity for people by using them as therapy dogs. Many facilities welcome therapy dogs to visit the elderly, disabled or sick. With little encouragement, the dogs enjoy making friends as long as their owners are by their sides when meeting patients in hospitals or residents in nursing homes or retirement centers. If you are interested in getting involved with therapy-dog work, contact Therapy Dogs International, Inc., online at www.tdi-dog.org.

A DOG OF CHARACTER

The Fédération Cynologique Internationale (FCI) translation of the breed standard of the Japan Dog Federation states, "Character: The temperamental quality should be of sagacity, cheerfulness and bravery, keen, sharp and high strung, having firmness of mind not to be an easy prey to temptation in addition to an alert watchfulness."

Despite claims that the breed was devised by breeding small Samoyeds, we know that this is not true. The Japanese Spitz is not a "small Samoyed" and does not act like a Samoyed. Where the Samoyed is bounding with power and pull, the Japanese Spitz is all sprint, spin and run. Owners will find it really quite amazing how fast and agile these dogs are.

Note also that the Japanese Spitz does not carry his tail in the fashion of the Samoyed. The Japanese Spitz carries his well-plumed tail in the center of his back, unlike the Samoyed that carries his plume to the side. Another difference is in coloration: The Japanese Spitz is pure white, while the Samoyed can be exhibited in white, cream and biscuit. In Russia, Samoyeds can also be seen in a variety of other colors; sometimes these are referred to as Nenets Herding Laikas. Of course, the Japanese Spitz and Samoyed, two perfectly

coated beauties, are both beloved for their ability to bond closely with their humans, yet with the Japanese Spitz there's a bit of a twist!

Although the Japanese Spitz is certainly very devoted to his owner and family, it is surprising how fickle he can be. This characteristic has pluses and minuses. While no owner wants to think of his dog as not truly loyal to him, it is a definite plus when the dog can adjust if his owner has to be away for long trips. Likewise, should Japanese Spitzen need to be rehomed for any reason, they appear to have no problems bonding to their new homes and owners very quickly. This is true even for the older dogs, 11 years plus.

The Japanese Spitz is a real home companion who thrives on

Biscuit markings, shown here, are unacceptable in the breed. The Japanese Spitz's coat must be pure white with no shadings.

The Japanese Spitz eye (top) is compared with the shape of the Gingko nut (bottom).

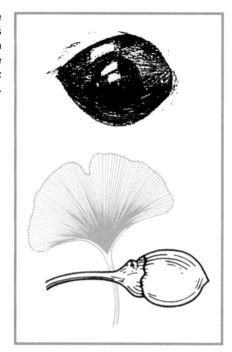

Tear stains, often seen on light-colored dogs, can be removed with a special cleanser made just for this purpose. If tear staining is excessive, you should discuss the problem with your veterinarian.

human company and is happiest when he's around his people. He is not suited to life in a kennel. Japanese Spitzen make ideal family pets and are very tolerant of children, with the exception of very young children who unknowingly "maul" the dog. Toddlers, therefore, should be supervised whenever in the company of the dog, so that the children do not grab at his coat and tail or otherwise abuse the dog, albeit unintentionally. Most children get along terrifically with the breed, as long as the child treats the dog gently, never too roughly or aggressively. The Japanese Spitz is an ideal breed for teenage owners, who seem to set up a rapport very quickly with their active, ready-to-go canine friend.

THAT AMAZING SPITZ COAT

Having come to Japan from the Arctic region, Japanese Spitzen are as much at home in the snow as they are in the tropics. Due to their well-insulated coats, neither heat nor cold bothers them. No matter how good your intentions of keeping your dog cool in the summer or your house "fur-free," *never shave your dog's coat.* You will cause irreparable damage to the coat. If you want a non-shedding dog, get a Poodle!

Note that most people do not have allergic reactions to the breed's hair, as they would with

Japanese Spitz hair is good for spinning into clothing, including scarves, hats, sweaters and the like. A pair of Japanese Spitzen poses by a loom on which this cardigan made of the breed's hair has been spun.

that of most other double-coated breeds. And better yet, the Japanese Spitz is one of the few breeds of dog that does not have a "doggy odor"—when dry or wet!

HEALTH CONSIDERATIONS
The Japanese Spitz is generally a healthy little dog, but, as in most breeds, certain health problems arise and new owners should be aware of these before committing to owning the breed.

KNEE PROBLEMS
Japanese Spitzen are known to suffer from trouble with the knee joints. This problem, known as patellar luxation, is usually associated with small dog breeds that have narrow leg bones. Some dogs with patellar problems do not suffer a great deal of pain but, with more severe cases, surgery is required. You should restrict your Japanese Spitz from too much jumping, stair climbing and similar stressful activities. Likewise, do not allow him to become overweight.

EYE PROBLEMS
Japanese Spitzen fairly frequently suffer from tear staining, which is caused by the eyes running and the tears not going down the tear ducts, thus leaving stains on the face. It is sometimes caused by the

The Japanese Spitz is known for being alert, keen and watchful, aptly illustrated by the intense concentration shown in this dog's expression.

ducts being closed, which can be checked and cleared by your vet. Another possible cause is an eye infection, which requires immediate attention by a vet.

HIP AND ELBOW DYSPLASIA
Although the breed is not known to have frequent occurrence of these orthopedic diseases, owners must be aware of the prominence of hip and elbow dysplasia in pure-bred dogs. Both diseases are hereditary and affect the dog's hips and elbows, respectively. They are caused by incorrectly formed joints, which become loose with use and eventually arthritic. Depending on the degree of the disease, the dog may live a normal life. In worst-case scenarios, a dog can be rendered lame. Discuss

dysplasia with your breeder. Many breeders have their dogs' hips and elbows screened and cleared of dysplasia before including them in a breeding program.

THE HEAT IS ON
The white coat of the Japanese Spitz reflects the heat of the sun, protecting the breed considerably from heat stroke. Dark-colored dogs, on the contrary, are at greater risk of suffering from heat exhaustion. The Japanese Spitz's dark pigment also protects the dog from sunburn. Precautions against heat stroke and sunburn, of course, are still advised. Provide your Japanese Spitz with an outdoor dog house or another suitable resting place to get away from the sun's rays on hot summer days.

DO YOU KNOW ABOUT HIP DYSPLASIA?

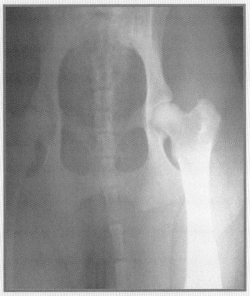

X-ray of a dog with "Good" hips.

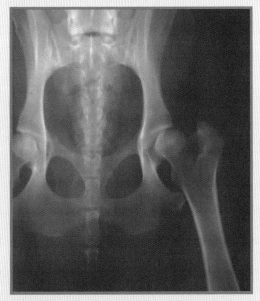

X-ray of a dog with "Moderate" dysplastic hips.

Hip dysplasia is a fairly common condition found in pure-bred dogs. When a dog has hip dysplasia, his hind leg has an incorrectly formed hip joint. By constant use of the hip joint, it becomes more and more loose, wears abnormally and may become arthritic.

Hip dysplasia can only be confirmed with an x-ray, but certain symptoms may indicate a problem. Your dog may have a hip dysplasia problem if he walks in a peculiar manner, hops instead of smoothly runs, uses his hind legs in unison (to keep the pressure off the weak joint), has trouble getting up from a prone position or always sits with both legs together on one side of his body.

As the dog matures, he may adapt well to life with a bad hip, but in a few years the arthritis develops. Many dogs with hip dysplasia eventually become crippled.

Hip dysplasia is considered an inherited disease and only can be diagnosed definitively by x-ray when the dog is two years old, although symptoms often appear earlier. Some experts claim that a special diet might help your puppy outgrow the bad hip, but the usual treatments are surgical. The removal of the pectineus muscle, the removal of the round part of the femur, reconstructing the pelvis and replacing the hip with an artificial one are all surgical interventions that are expensive, but they are usually very successful. Follow the advice of your veterinarian.

BREED STANDARD FOR THE

JAPANESE SPITZ

INTRODUCTION TO THE BREED STANDARD

Each breed of dog has a breed standard, a picture in words of the ideal specimen of the breed in looks, temperament and movement. Breed standards are formulated differently in each country. In England, The Kennel Club controls breed standards with input from the various breed clubs. Breed clubs have members who are owners and breeders, who have a great deal of interest and knowledge in their breed and who have studied their individual breed over a number of years. Once the club members have agreed on what the standard should contain, discussions then take place between the club and the Standards sub-committee of The Kennel Club.

Each British standard is made up of a series of headings (points of the dog). These headings are the same for each breed of dog. When content of a standard is agreed upon, it goes before the General Committee of The Kennel Club for final ratification. The KC

also decides in which of the seven groups the breed should be placed (Working, Toy, Utility, etc.), and then publishes the standard.

In the United States, the standard is devised by the breed's parent club, without input from the American Kennel Club. Once the parent club's membership agrees upon the standard, it is then sent to the AKC for acceptance.

The Fédération Cynologique Internationale (FCI) accepts standards for dog breeds worldwide; each standard is based on the dog's country of origin. Of course, the FCI standard could be different from the English or American standards, depending on the breed and its country of origin. For example, the British standard for the Japanese Spitz differs slightly in wording from that of the FCI.

In the UK, the Japanese Spitz is a member of the Utility Group; in Europe, the breed is included in Group 5 for spitz and primitive-type dogs. First let us look at the FCI standard, which is

A Japanese Spitz dog in profile, showing correct type, structure and balance with a full mature coat.

based on that of the Japan Dog Federation, and then we will examine the British standard. Study of these standards will help the reader to better understand the ideal Japanese Spitz.

FCI STANDARD FOR THE JAPANESE SPITZ

Origin: Japan.

Date of Publication: 1997.

Utilization: Companion dog.

FCI Classification: Group 5: Spitz and primitive types; Section 5: Asian spitz and related breeds.

General Appearance: Covered with profuse pure white coat, with pointed muzzle, triangular pricked ears, and feathered tail over back. The constitution tough and the whole well balanced, and its harmonious beauty causing spirit and dignity peculiar to this breed, and expressing elegance.

Important Proportions: The ratio of height at withers to length of body is 10:11.

Temperament: Intelligent, cheerful, keen in sense. Noisy not permitted.

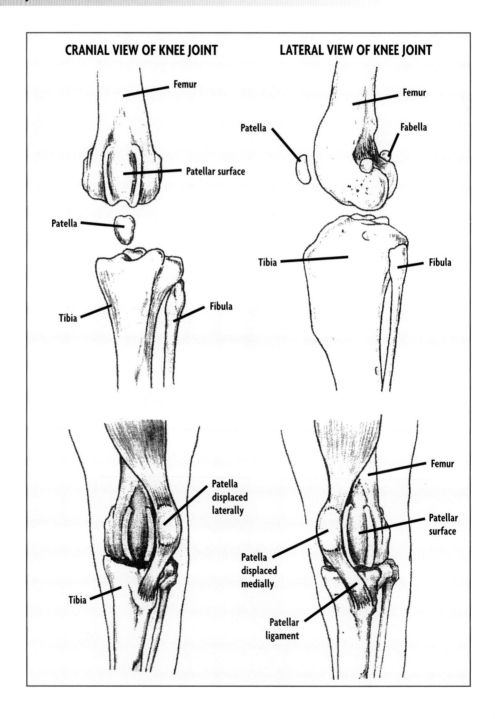

CRANIAL VIEW OF KNEE JOINT

Femur

Patellar surface

Patella

Tibia

Fibula

Patella displaced laterally

Tibia

LATERAL VIEW OF KNEE JOINT

Femur

Patella

Fabella

Tibia

Fibula

Femur

Patellar surface

Patella displaced medially

Patellar ligament

Head: Size in harmony with body and moderately broad and rounded.

Cranial Region: Skull: Rear part of skull broadest. Stop: Defined.

Facial Region: The forehead moderately developed. Nose: Small, round and black. Muzzle: Pointed, the tip slightly round, and well balanced. Lips tight and preferably black. Teeth: White and strong with scissors bite. Eyes: Moderately large, almond-shaped, set slightly oblique, dark in color. Black eyerims. Ears: Set on high, small, triangular, pricked, facing forward, and not too far apart. Neck: Moderately long, muscles well developed.

Body: *Withers:* High. *Back:* Straight and short. *Loins:* Broad. *Chest:* Wide and deep, ribs well sprung. *Belly:* Well drawn up. *Tail:* Set on high, moderately long, carried over back.

Limbs: *Forequarters:* Shoulders well sloping, forearms straight, elbows tight.

Hindquarters: Muscular, stifle and hock moderately bent.

Feet: Cat feet. Pads thick, and desirably black as well as the nails.

Gait: Quick and active.

Coat: *Hair:* Outer coat straight and stand-off. Undercoat short, soft

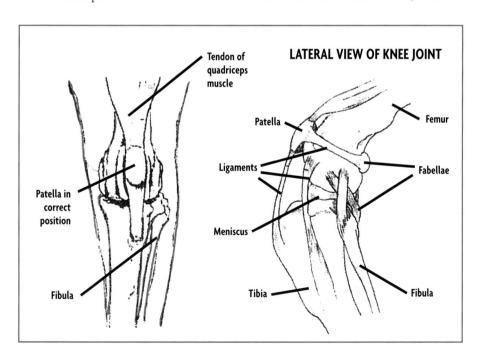

LATERAL VIEW OF KNEE JOINT

Tendon of quadriceps muscle

Patella in correct position

Fibula

Patella

Ligaments

Meniscus

Tibia

Femur

Fabellae

Fibula

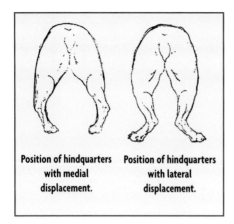

Position of hindquarters with medial displacement.   Position of hindquarters with lateral displacement.

and dense. The foreface, ears, front of forearms and parts below hocks are short-haired, and the rest covered with abundant long hair, especially from neck to shoulders and forechest covered with beautiful frill, and the tail also has long, profuse feathering.

Color: Pure white.

Size: *Height at withers:* Dogs 30–38 cm; bitches slightly smaller than dogs.

Correct profile.

Too much stop.

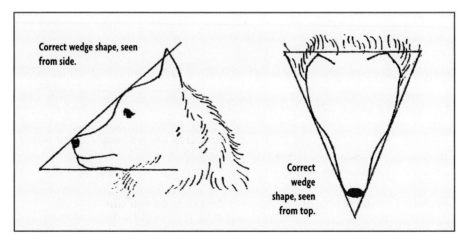

Correct wedge shape, seen from side.

Correct wedge shape, seen from top.

A LOOK AT THE ENGLISH STANDARD

The following is an amplification of the English Kennel Club's standard.

General Appearance: The importance of the profuse pure white coat (not allowing biscuit or any other shading) is most essential for the overall picture of the breed. To obtain the desired firm body, strength and flexibility, the Japanese Spitz must be a sturdy dog, not at all like a toy breed. The height-to-length ratio of 10:11 indicates that a square outline is not required.

Characteristics: Affectionate and companionable well describes how the dogs are with their families. They are not extroverted and can be slightly chary with strangers; as is the Oriental custom, they like to be introduced. This is not to be interpreted as a sign of aggression, hostility or nervousness; it is simply caution.

Temperament: They are alert and intelligent, but in a different way than sheepdogs and other working dogs. They are eager to please.

Head and Skull: Muzzle pointed, neither too thick nor too long, a triangle should be formed between the outside of the ears, down the face, passing just on the

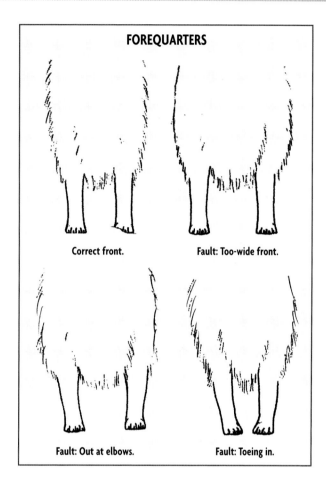

FOREQUARTERS

Correct front.

Fault: Too-wide front.

Fault: Out at elbows.

Fault: Toeing in.

outside edge of the eyes to the outside of the nose. The well-balanced head is equidistant from the nose to the stop and from the stop to the back of the skull. It is essential that the nose and lips are jet black; it is a fault to have "winter nose" (pink pigmentation).

Eyes: Although the original Japanese standard called for

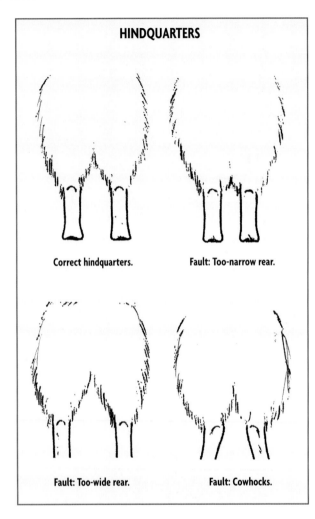

HINDQUARTERS

Correct hindquarters.

Fault: Too-narrow rear.

Fault: Too-wide rear.

Fault: Cowhocks.

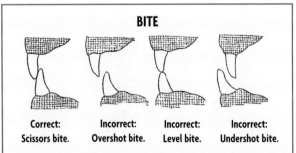

BITE

Correct: Scissors bite.

Incorrect: Overshot bite.

Incorrect: Level bite.

Incorrect: Undershot bite.

Head study showing a Japanese Spitz head of correct type, structure and proportion with proper dark pigment.

"Gingko nut shape," the term "almond-shape" was substituted for the simple reason that the Gingko nut was not well known in Europe. Since the Gingko and almond have completely different shapes, this substitution was deemed incorrect, and the current standard uses the term "oval," which is a lot nearer the shape of the Gingko. The eyes should be dark; a light eye is to be frowned upon.

Ears: Small, teddy-bear-like, standing upright and triangular in shape, the ears can be mobile, giving a varied and pleasing range of expressions. They should be forward-facing.

Faults: Large, wide-set ears with rounded tips; eyes too large, round and light in color; poor pigment on eyerims, nose and lips.

Mouth: The dog's mouth should have good, strong white teeth, of the correct number, set square to the jaw, forming a regular scissors bite (that is, upper teeth closely overlapping the lower teeth).

Neck: This should be strong, arched and of moderate length. The arch and length give the dog a look of quality and alertness; a short neck gives the dog a look of weariness and boredom.

Forequarters: The combination of the arch of the neck and well-laid shoulders gives the Japanese Spitz a desired pleasant sweep to the topline. Note, also, that the forelegs are straight, with slightly sloping pasterns.

Body: The standard calls for the back to be straight and short,

FAULTS IN PROFILE

Faults: Narrow front, upright shoulders, high in rear, insufficient rear angulation, low on leg.

Faults: Long back, too wide in front, toes out in front.

Faults: Flat-lying sparse coat, lacking bone and substance, weak pasterns, flat feet, upright shoulders, narrow rear, lacking adequate angulation.

which would seem to conflict with the 10:11 height-length ratio. This ratio is of great importance, ensuring that the back is not too short. Regarding "bone," the

standard does not mention that fine bone would make the dog look toyish and frail, or that too heavy bone makes a cloddy animal. Although not stated in the standard, the bone needs to be moderately heavy.

Hindquarters: The standard calls for muscular hindquarters, enabling the dog to move with drive. The feet should be small, round and cat-like, free of feathering.

Tail: This is one of the breed's most lovely features, profusely covered with long hair and curled over the back. The set of the tail must be high so that it can be carried in a curl on top of the back. It should not drop to the side, Samoyed-style, nor should it be too tightly curled.

Gait: The breed's movement should be very smooth. The Japanese Spitz should not

prance. When moving correctly, the dog uses his well-muscled hindquarters to drive him over the ground.

Coat: The standard states that the outer coat is straight and stand-off with a profuse, short, dense undercoat, which is soft in texture. The coat is shorter on the face, the ears, the front of the limbs and below the hocks. The mane is impressive, reaching down to the brisket.

Color: The Japanese Spitz is pure white, with no shadings. Unlike the Samoyed, the breed is not allowed in cream or biscuit.

Size: When the breed was first imported into the UK, the standard called for dogs to be 12–16 inches and bitches to be 10–14 inches. Breeders felt that there was far too wide a range between the bigger dogs and the smaller bitches, so the standard was revised to say dogs 30–36 cm (12–14 inches) and bitches slightly smaller. The wording of "bitches slightly smaller" still causes some concern, as some bitches are still too small. Dogs and bitches in the larger end of the size range appear to be far more sound and have better thickness of bone.

Judges at dog shows use the breed standard as a guideline for determining the quality of the dogs being shown. Although standards around the world describe the same basic dog, the standard used depends on the country in which the show takes place.

JAPANESE SPITZ

SELECTING A PUPPY

After learning about the breed's character, history and appearance, you have decided that the Japanese Spitz is the breed for you. You will not be disappointed by this remarkable companion dog, but how do you find a Japanese Spitz? Good question. Regardless of which country you live in, the search for a Japanese Spitz will require some research and fancy footwork. You will not find pages of advertisements in the dog magazines because this is a rare breed that has a very limited (but dedicated!) following at this point in time. That is not all bad! Unlike overly popular breeds like the Labrador Retriever, Border Collie and German Shepherd, the Japanese Spitz does not suffer from profiteering dealers trying to sell unsound, unhealthy puppies. The breeders that you find for Japanese Spitzen should be dedicated to the breed and, ideally, knowledgeable about dogs in general and the breed in specific.

PUPPY APPEARANCE

Your puppy should have a well-fed appearance but not a distended abdomen, which may indicate worms or incorrect feeding, or both. The body should be firm, with a solid feel. The skin of the abdomen should be pale pink and clean, without signs of scratching or rash. Check the legs to see if the dewclaws have been removed, as this is done at just a few weeks old.

Here are some of the ways to find a litter of Japanese Spitz puppies:

1. Contact the secretary or registrar of the national breed club (such as England's Japanese Spitz Club).
2. Contact the national kennel club, which should have information about puppies available by breed. In the UK, the English Kennel Club will be of assistance. Europeans will rely upon the Fédération Cynologique Internationale (FCI). Although the American Kennel Club does not recognize the Japanese Spitz, residents of the US have other options: contact the American Rare Breed Association, the Continental Kennel Club, the National Kennel Club, the States Kennel Club or the United Kennel Club. All of these are all-breed registries that hold shows and keep track of dogs in hundreds of breeds.
3. Check in dog magazines and the weekly published dog papers. In Britain, *Our Dogs* and *Dog World* (UK); in the US, *Dog Fancy* and *Dog World*.
4. Go to dog shows where the breed is represented and meet the exhibitors.
5. Your local vet may be able to help with referrals.
6 The Internet is a fabulous source of information on rare breeds, but always beware that there are some unscrupulous advertisers using this media.

MEETING THE LITTER

Having found a reputable breeder with a litter of Japanese Spitzen, make arrangements to go and meet the puppies as soon as possible. The puppies will be at least five

---

PEDIGREE VS. REGISTRATION CERTIFICATE

Too often new owners are confused between these two important documents. Your puppy's pedigree, essentially a family tree, is a written record of a dog's genealogy of three generations or more. The pedigree will show you the names as well as performance titles of all dogs in your pup's background. Your breeder must provide you with a registration application, with his part properly filled out. You must complete the application and send it to the registering kennel club. In the US, an owner has several choices of organizations with which to register his Japanese Spitz, likely based on with whom the breeder's dogs are registered.

The seller must provide you with complete records to identify the puppy. The AKC requires that the seller provide the buyer with the following: breed; sex, color and markings; date of birth; litter number (when available); names and registration numbers of the parents; breeder's name; and date sold or delivered.

weeks of age before the breeder allows visitors, and they can leave for new homes around eight to ten weeks of age. They will be indescribably irresistible balls of white fur. Easy does it! When you arrive at the breeder's home (and before you are seduced by the litter), look around to see how clean the premises are. Note if there are places where the puppies can be alone to rest and sleep. Or, are they crowded in a small cluttered corner (*not* a good sign)?

When you first see the puppies, they should all run towards you, wanting to be fussed over. They should all be about the same size—nice, round, plump bundles of white fur. Be wary of the one that stays in the corner away from the others or one that is smaller or thin. Look at their eyes to see if any of them have runny or red bloodshot eyes; they should be bright and sparkling. If, while you are there, any pup

Get ready to add a "baby" to the family. Many owners enjoy pampering and showing off their beautiful Japanese Spitzen, and the breed's small size makes it easy.

ARE YOU PREPARED?
Unfortunately, when a puppy is bought by someone who does not take into consideration the time and attention that dog ownership requires, it is the puppy who suffers when he is either abandoned or placed in a shelter by a frustrated owner. So all of the "homework" you do in preparation for your pup's arrival will benefit you both. The more informed you are, the more you will know what to expect and the better equipped you will be to handle the ups and downs of raising a puppy. Hopefully, everyone in the household is willing to do his part in raising and caring for the pup. The anticipation of owning a dog often brings a lot of promises from excited family members: "I will walk him every day," "I will feed him," "I will house-train him," etc., but these things take time and effort, and promises can easily be forgotten once the novelty of the new pet has worn off.

passes motions, note that the stool should be dark and firm (never runny or grayish).

Ask the breeder to let you see the litter's sire and dam. The parents will give you a good idea of what the puppies' future temperament will be like. It is possible (even likely) that the sire does not live with the breeder, but the dam should always be on the premises, available for you to meet.

Watch how the pups move. It should be easy to see them move straight on well-boned legs. Beware of the puppy that keeps falling over or whose legs do not move smoothly. Remember to ask the breeder if you can see copies of the parents' patellar clearances, which should have been obtained from their own vets. If the breeder cannot supply these (or claims that they are not necessary, etc.), consider seriously going to another breeder, no matter how adorable the puppies are!

The puppies' ears should be erect by the time the puppies are eight weeks of age, but this is not always so. Ears vary from pup to pup, so this not so critical at this young age. If you are purchasing your Japanese Spitz puppy for future show purposes, you might want to wait until the pup is 10 to 12 weeks of age and so that you are sure about erect ears, dropped testicles, etc.

Ask the breeder if there were or are any problems with the health of the parents or grandparents. A breeder who is interested in the breed should answer these questions honestly and should be glad that you are concerned and well informed. Ask when the pups were last wormed. If one of the puppies melts your heart, pick him up for a closer examination. He should have a sweet smell; his

TEMPERAMENT COUNTS

Your selection of a good puppy can be determined by your needs. A show potential or a good pet? It is your choice. Every puppy, however, should be of good temperament. Although show-quality puppies are bred and raised with emphasis on physical conformation, responsible breeders strive for equally good temperament. Do not buy from a breeder who concentrates solely on physical beauty at the expense of personality.

eyes should be bright and not running, with no signs of tear staining; his nose should be cool and moist. He should cuddle into you and appear happy and contented, but he should also be inquisitive.

When you have decided on which puppy is the right one for you, check with the breeder about

The following photos, viewed counterclockwise, document the development of puppies bred by the author through artificial insemination.

Pups at 9 days old.

Pups at 14 days old.

Pups at 17 days old.

the registration, insurance, health guarantee, documentation of wormings and inoculations, pedigree, diet sheet, sales contract and receipt. The breeder will allow you 24 hours (or more) to take the puppy to the vet for a complete examination. Make certain that the breeder will return your money or allow you to select another puppy if the vet advises you not to keep the puppy due to health problems.

Keep in mind that you will likely pay more for a rare-breed puppy than you will for an average pure-bred dog. Prices vary depending on the breeder, but you should never settle for a "bargain puppy" because you will pay for it over and over again at the vet's office—not to mention the incalculable costs of your broken heart when the puppy succumbs to an illness or has to be put down for an unsound temperament.

Pup at 4 weeks old.

PREPARING PUPPY'S PLACE IN YOUR HOME

Researching your breed and finding a breeder are only two aspects of the "homework" you will have to do before bringing your Japanese Spitz puppy home. You will also have to prepare your home and family for the new addition. Much as you would prepare a nursery for a newborn baby, you will need to designate a place in your home that will be the puppy's own. How you prepare your home will depend on how much freedom the dog will be allowed. Whatever you decide, you must ensure that he has a place that he can "call his own."

When you bring your new puppy into your home, you are bringing him into what will become his home as well. Obviously, you did not buy a puppy with the intentions of catering to his every whim and

Pups at 14 weeks old.

Pup at 10 weeks old.

Pup at 5 weeks old.

Pups at 8 weeks old.

Your local pet shop will carry a range of crates, from which you can choose one suitable for your Japanese Spitz. Get one from the start that will comfortably house your dog at his full adult size.

allowing him to "rule the roost," but in order for a puppy to grow into a stable, well-adjusted dog, he has to feel comfortable in his surroundings. Remember, he is leaving the warmth and security of his dam and littermates, as well as the familiarity of the only place he has ever known, so it is important to make his transition as easy as possible. By preparing a

place in your home for the puppy, you are making him feel as welcome as possible in a strange new place. Your puppy should warm up to his new environs in no time at all.

WHAT YOU SHOULD BUY

CRATE

To someone unfamiliar with the use of crates in dog training, it may seem like punishment to shut a dog in a crate, but this is not the case at all. More and more breeders and trainers worldwide are recommending crates as preferred tools for pet puppies as well as show puppies.

Crates are not cruel—crates have many humane and highly effective uses in dog care and training. For example, crate training is a popular and very successful house-training method. In addition, a crate can keep your dog safe during travel and, perhaps most importantly, a crate provides your dog with a place of his own in your home. It serves as a "doggie bedroom" of sorts—your Japanese Spitz can curl up in his crate when he wants to sleep or when he just needs a break. Many dogs sleep in their crates overnight. With soft bedding and his favorite toy, a crate becomes a cozy pseudo-den for your dog. Like his ancestors, he too will seek out the comfort and retreat of a den—you just happen to be

A large wire pen with a bowl of fresh water creates a safe environment in which your puppy can enjoy some time outdoors.

providing him with something a little more luxurious than what his early ancestors enjoyed.

As far as purchasing a crate, the type that you buy is up to you. It will most likely be one of the two most popular types: wire or fiberglass. There are advantages and disadvantages to each type.

For example, a wire crate is more open, allowing the air to flow through and affording the dog a view of what is going on around him. Wire crates are good for use in the home. Fiberglass crates are sturdier and are usually the crates of choice for traveling, although both types can double as travel

Left: Make your puppy's introduction to his crate pleasant. At first, with you supervising, leave the door open and let him explore the crate and enter and exit as he wishes. Right: Your puppy may be a bit fidgety at first, but soon he will settle down and become comfortable.

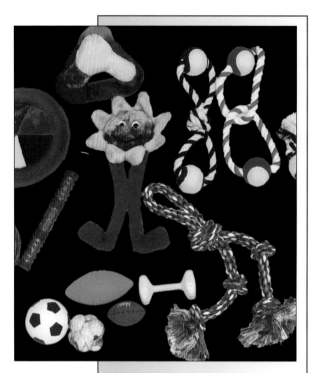

TOYS, TOYS, TOYS!
With a big variety of dog toys available, and so many that look like they would be a lot of fun for a dog, be careful in your selection. It is amazing what a set of puppy teeth can do to an innocent-looking toy, so, obviously, safety is a major considera-tion. Be sure to choose the most durable products that you can find. Hard nylon bones and toys are a safe bet, and many of them are offered in different scents and flavors that will be sure to capture your dog's attention. It is always fun to play a game of fetch with your dog, and there are balls and flying discs that are specially made to withstand dog teeth.

crates, providing protection for the dog in the car.

The size of the crate is another thing to consider. The Japanese Spitz will require a crate that is at least 19 x 24 x 22 inches, giving him enough room as an adult to stand up, lie down and be comfortable.

BEDDING
A soft crate pad and a cuddly blanket in your Japanese Spitz's crate will make the crate more comfortable and will help the dog feel at home. First, these things will take the place of the leaves, twigs, etc., that the pup would use in the wild to make a den; the pup can make his own "burrow" in the crate. Although your pup is far removed from his den-making ancestors, the denning instinct is still a part of his genetic makeup. Second, until you take your pup home, he has been sleeping amid the warmth of his dam and litter-mates, and while a blanket is not the same as a warm, breathing body, it still provides heat and something with which to snuggle. You will want to wash your pup's bedding frequently in case he has a potty "accident" in his crate, and replace or remove anything in his crate that becomes ragged and starts to fall apart.

TOYS
Toys are a must for dogs of all ages, especially for curious

playful pups. Puppies are the "children" of the dog world, and what child does not love toys? Chew toys provide enjoyment for both dog and owner—your dog will enjoy playing with his favorite toys, while you will enjoy the fact that they distract him from chewing on your expensive shoes and leather sofa. Puppies love to chew; in fact, chewing is a physical need for pups as they are teething, and everything looks appetizing! Everything in your home is fair game in the eyes of a teething pup. Puppies are not all that discerning when it comes to finding something literally to "sink their teeth into"— everything tastes great!

Japanese Spitz are not known for being aggressive chewers. Any standard toys made for dogs should be suitable, but just use common sense in the toys that you offer. The author has found that his dogs welcome toy balls, rope pulls and cuddly squeaky toys.

Be careful of natural bones, which have a tendency to splinter into sharp, dangerous pieces. Also be careful of rawhide, which can turn into pieces that are easy to swallow and become a mushy mess on your carpet.

The best thing to do is to supervise your Japanese Spitz when he's playing with any potentially destructible toys, and offer him safe sturdy chews, such as hard nylon bones, for free play. Always keep a close eye on your dog's toys so that he doesn't swallow any of the stuffing from inside a toy or get a squeaker stuck in this throat. Monitor the condition of all of your pup's toys carefully and get rid of any that have been chewed to the point of becoming potentially dangerous.

PLAY'S THE THING

Teaching the puppy to play with his toys in running and fetching games is an ideal way to help the puppy develop muscle, learn motor skills and bond with you, his owner and master. He also needs to learn how to inhibit his bite reflex and never to use his teeth on people, forbidden objects and other animals in play. Whenever you play with your puppy, you make the rules. This becomes an important message to your puppy in teaching him that you are the pack leader and control everything he does in life. Once your dog accepts you as his leader, your relationship with him will be cemented for life.

Your puppy will need a lightweight yet sturdy leash to help him get accustomed to on-lead walking.

LEASH

A nylon leash is probably the best option, as it is the most resistant to puppy teeth should your pup take a liking to chewing on his leash. Of course, this is a habit that should be nipped in the bud, but, if your pup likes to chew on his leash, he has a very slim chance of being able to chew through the strong nylon. Nylon leashes are also lightweight, which is good for a young Japanese Spitz who is just getting used to the idea of walking on a leash. For everyday walking and safety purposes, the nylon leash is a good choice.

As your pup grows up and gets used to walking on the leash, and can do it politely, you may want to purchase a flexible leash. These leashes allow you to extend the length to give the dog a broader area to explore or to shorten the length to keep the dog near you.

COLLAR

Your pup should get used to wearing a collar all the time since you will want to attach his ID tags to it; plus, you have to attach the leash to something! A lightweight nylon collar is a good choice. Make certain that the collar fits snugly enough so that the pup cannot wriggle out of it, but is loose enough so that it will not be uncomfortably tight around the pup's neck. Keep in mind that the

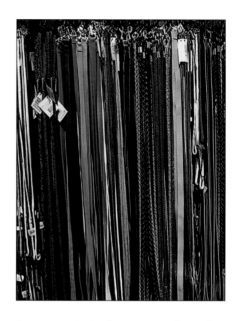

Japanese Spitz has quite a bit of hair growing around his neck! You should be able to fit two fingers between the pup's neck and the collar. It may take some time for your pup to get used to wearing the collar, but soon he will not even notice that it is there.

Choke collars are made for training, but are not recommended for use on small dogs and coated breeds, and therefore are doubly unsuitable for the Japanese Spitz.

FOOD AND WATER BOWLS

Your pup will need two bowls, one for food and one for water. You may want two sets of bowls, one for indoors and one for outdoors, depending on where

CHOOSE AN APPROPRIATE COLLAR

The **BUCKLE COLLAR** is the standard collar used for everyday purposes. Be sure that you adjust the buckle on growing puppies. Check it every day. It can become too tight overnight! These collars can be made of leather or nylon. Attach your dog's identification tags to this collar.

The **CHOKE COLLAR** is designed for training. It is constructed of highly polished steel so that it slides easily through the stainless steel loop. The idea is that the dog controls the pressure around his neck and he will stop pulling if the collar becomes uncomfortable. This type of collar should not be used on the Japanese Spitz, as it is not appropriate for small dogs and also can pull and damage long coats.

The **HALTER** is for a trained dog that has to be restrained to prevent running away, chasing a cat and the like. Considered the most humane of all collars, it is frequently used on smaller dogs on which collars are not comfortable.

Photo courtesy of Mikki Pet Products.

the dog will be fed and where he will be spending time. Stainless steel or sturdy plastic bowls are popular choices. Plastic bowls are more chewable, but dogs tend not to chew on the steel variety, which can be sterilized. It is important to buy sturdy bowls since anything is in danger of being chewed by puppy teeth and you do not want your dog to be constantly chewing apart his bowl (for his safety and for your purse!).

CLEANING SUPPLIES

Until a pup is house-trained, you will be doing a lot of cleaning. "Accidents" will occur, which is acceptable in the beginning stages of toilet training because the puppy does not know any better. All you can do is be prepared to clean up any accidents as soon as they happen. Old rags, paper towels, newspapers and a safe disinfectant are good to have.

BEYOND THE BASICS

The items previously discussed are the bare necessities. You will find out what else you need as you go along—grooming supplies, flea/tick protection, baby gates to partition a room, etc. These things will vary depending on your situation, but it is important that you have everything you need to feed and make your Japanese Spitz comfortable in his first few days at home.

PUPPY-PROOFING YOUR HOME

Aside from making sure that your Japanese Spitz will be comfortable in your home, you also have to make sure that your home is safe for your Japanese Spitz. This means taking precautions that your pup will not get into anything he should not get into and that there is nothing within his reach that may harm him should he sniff it, chew it, inspect it, etc. This probably seems obvious since, while you are primarily concerned with your pup's safety, at the same time you do not want your belongings to be ruined. Breakables should be placed out of reach if your dog is to have full run of the house. If he is to be limited to certain places within the house, keep any potentially dangerous items in the "off-limits" areas.

An electrical cord can pose a danger should the puppy decide to taste it—and who is going to convince a pup that it would not make a great chew toy? All cords and wires should be fastened tightly against the wall and kept from puppy's reach and teeth. If your Japanese Spitz is going to spend time in a crate, make sure that there is nothing near his crate that he can reach if he sticks his curious little nose or paws through the openings. Just as you would with a child, keep all household cleaners and chemicals where the pup cannot reach them.

It is your responsibility to clean up after your dog has relieved himself. Pet shops have various aids to assist in the cleanup job.

It is also important to make sure that the outside of your home is safe. Of course, your puppy should never be unsupervised, but a pup let loose in the yard will want to run and explore, and he should be granted that freedom. Do not let a fence give you a false sense of security; you would be surprised at how crafty (and persistent) a dog can be in figuring out how to dig under and squeeze his way through small holes, or to jump or climb over a fence.

The Japanese Spitz is an excellent jumper. Many Japanese Spitzen are capable of jumping as high as 4 feet straight in the air. Keep the Japanese Spitz's jumping ability in mind when enclosing your property. The fence must be

NATURAL TOXINS

Examine your grass and landscaping before bringing your puppy home. Many varieties of plants have leaves, stems or flowers that are toxic if ingested, and you can depend on a curious puppy to investigate them. Ask your vet for information on poisonous plants or research them at your library.

If you see your dog carrying a piece of vegetation in his mouth, approach him in a quiet, disinterested manner, avoid eye contact, pet him and gradually remove the plant from his mouth. Alternatively, offer him a treat and maybe he'll drop the plant on his own accord. Be sure no toxic plants are growing in your own yard or kept in your home.

high enough so that it really is impossible for your Japanese Spitz to get over it; a height of at least 5 feet is necessary.

Some Japanese Spitzen enjoy digging, and the art of escape is dear to most members of the spitz family. Thus, the fence should be embedded at least a foot into the ground. Be sure to secure any gaps in the fence. Check the fence periodically to ensure that it is in good shape and make repairs as needed. A very determined (or very bored) pup may return to the same spot to "work on it" until he is able to get through.

FIRST TRIP TO THE VET

You have selected your puppy, and your home and family are ready. Now all you have to do is collect your Japanese Spitz from the breeder and the fun begins, right? Well...not so fast. Something else you need to plan is your pup's first trip to the veterinarian. Perhaps your breeder can recommend someone in the area who specializes in spitz-type breeds, or maybe you know some other dog owners who can suggest a good vet. Either way, you should have an appointment arranged for your pup before you pick him up.

The pup's first visit will consist of an overall examination to make sure that the pup does not have any problems that are not apparent to you. The vet will also set up a schedule for the pup's vaccinations; the breeder will inform you of which ones the pup has already received and the vet can continue from there.

INTRODUCTION TO THE FAMILY

Everyone in the house will be excited about the puppy's coming home and will want to pet him and play with him, but it is best to keep the introductions low-key so as not to overwhelm the puppy. He is apprehensive already. It is the first time he has been separated from his dam and the breeder, and the ride to your home is likely to be the first time he has been in a car. The last thing you want to do is smother him, as this will only frighten him further. This is not to say that human contact is not extremely necessary at this stage, because this is the time when a connection between the pup and his human family is formed. Gentle petting and soothing words should help console him, as well as just putting him down and letting him explore on his own (under your watchful eye, of course).

The pup may approach the family members or may busy himself with exploring for a while. Gradually, each person should spend some time with the pup, one at a time, crouching down to get as close to the pup's level as possible while letting him

SKULL & CROSSBONES
Thoroughly puppy-proof your house before bringing your puppy home. Never use cockroach or rodent poisons or plant fertilizers in any area accessible to the puppy. Avoid the use of toilet cleaners. Most dogs are born with "toilet-bowl sonar" and will take a drink if the lid is left open. Also keep the trash secured and out of reach.

Scour your garage for potential puppy dangers. Remove weed killers, pesticides and antifreeze materials. Antifreeze is highly toxic and just a few drops can kill a puppy or an adult dog. The sweet taste attracts the animal, who will quickly consume it from the floor or pavement.

sniff their hands and petting him gently. He definitely needs human attention and he needs to be touched—this is how to form an immediate bond. Just remember that the pup is experiencing many

This Japanese Spitz has private transportation and even his own personal tour guide to show him around his new backyard.

Once he's adjusted to his new home and family, your Japanese Spitz's true happy nature will shine through.

and the family cat. He's explored his area, his new bed, the yard and anywhere else he's been permitted. He's eaten his first meal at home and relieved himself in the proper place. He's heard lots of new sounds, smelled new friends and seen more of the outside world than ever before…and that was just the first day! He's worn out and is ready for bed…or so you think!

It's puppy's first night home and you are ready to say "Good night." Keep in mind that this is his first night ever to be sleeping alone. His dam and littermates are no longer at paw's length and he's a bit scared, cold and lonely. Be reassuring to your new family member, but this is not the time to spoil him and give in to his inevitable whining.

Puppies whine. They whine to let others know where they are and hopefully to get company out of it. Place your pup in his new bed or crate in his designated area and close the crate door. Mercifully, he may fall asleep

things for the first time, at the same time. There are new people, new noises, new smells and new things to investigate, so be gentle, be affectionate and be as comforting as you can be.

PUP'S FIRST NIGHT HOME

You have traveled home with your new charge safely in his crate. He's been to the vet for a thorough check-up; he's been weighed, his papers have been examined and perhaps he's even been vaccinated and wormed as well. He's met the whole family, including the excited children

---

IN DUE TIME

It will take at least two weeks for your puppy to become accustomed to his new surroundings. Give him lots of love, attention, handling, frequent opportunities to relieve himself, a diet he likes to eat and a place he can call his own.

Unless you want to play with your pup every night at 10 p.m., midnight and 2 a.m., don't initiate the habit. Your family will thank you, and eventually so will your pup!

PREVENTING PUPPY PROBLEMS

SOCIALIZATION

Now that you have done all of the preparatory work and have helped your pup get accustomed to his

without a peep. When the inevitable occurs, however, ignore the whining—he is fine. Be strong and keep his interest in mind. Do not allow yourself to feel guilty and visit the pup. He will fall asleep eventually.

Many breeders recommend placing a piece of bedding from the pup's former home in his new bed so that he recognizes and is comforted by the scent of his littermates. Others still advise placing a hot water bottle in the bed for warmth. The latter may be a good idea provided the pup doesn't attempt to suckle—he'll get good and wet, and may not fall asleep so fast.

Puppy's first night can be somewhat stressful for both the pup and his new family. Remember that you are setting the tone of nighttime at your house.

Future show stars start preparing for the ring early in life. Focusing on a treat certainly makes a pup stand at attention.

PUP MEETS WORLD

Thorough socialization includes not only meeting new people but also being introduced to new experiences such as riding in the car, having his coat brushed, hearing the television, walking in a crowd—the list is endless. The more your pup experiences, and the more positive the experiences are, the less of a shock and the less frightening it will be for your pup to encounter new things.

snowball that people will want to pet and, in general, think is absolutely precious! People will be charmed by your intriguing rare-breed pup, as he likely will be the only Japanese Spitz in the neighborhood (perhaps even in town!).

Besides getting to know his new family, your puppy should be exposed to other people, animals and situations. This will help him become well adjusted as he grows up and less prone to being timid or fearful of the new things he will encounter. Of course, he must not come into close contact with dogs you don't know well until his course of injections is fully complete.

Your pup's socialization began with the breeder, but now it is your responsibility to continue it. The socialization he receives until the age of 12 weeks is the most critical, as this is the time when he forms his impressions of the outside world. Be especially careful during the eight-to-ten-week-old period, also known as the fear period. The interaction he receives during this time should be gentle and reassuring. Lack of socialization, and/or negative experiences during the socialization period, can manifest itself in fear and aggression as the dog grows up; shyness and over-wariness of strangers also can be problems in a Japanese Spitz that has not been properly socialized.

new home and family, it is about time for you to have some fun! Socializing your Japanese Spitz pup gives you the opportunity to show off your new friend, and your pup gets to reap the benefits of being an adorable furry

Your puppy needs lots of positive interaction, which of course includes human contact, affection, handling and exposure to other animals.

Once your pup has received his necessary vaccinations, feel free to take him out and about (on his leash, of course). Walk him around the neighborhood, take him on your daily errands, let people pet him, let him meet other dogs and pets, etc. Puppies do not have to try to make friends; there will be no shortage of people who will want to introduce themselves. Just make sure that you carefully supervise each meeting. If the neighborhood children want to say hello, for example, that is great—children and pups most often make great companions. However, sometimes an excited child can unintention-ally handle a pup too roughly, or an overzealous pup can playfully nip a little too hard. You want to make socialization experiences positive ones. What a pup learns during this very formative stage will affect his attitude toward future encounters. You want your dog to be comfortable around everyone. A pup that has a bad experience with a child may grow up to be a dog that is shy around or aggressive toward children.

CONSISTENCY IN TRAINING
Dogs, being pack animals, naturally need a leader, or else

MANNERS MATTER
During the socialization process, a puppy should meet people, experience different environments and definitely be exposed to other canines. Through playing and interacting with other dogs, your puppy will learn lessons, ranging from controlling the pressure of his jaws by biting his littermates to the inner-workings of the canine pack that he will apply to his human relationships for the rest of his life. That is why removing a puppy from the litter too early can be detrimental to the pup's development.

TRAINING TIP
Training your puppy takes much patience and can be frustrating at times, but you should see results from your efforts. If you have a puppy that seems untrainable, take him to a trainer or behaviorist. The dog may have a personality problem that requires the help of a professional, or perhaps you need help in learning how to train your dog.

they try to establish dominance in their packs. When you welcome a dog into your family, the choice of who becomes the leader and who becomes the "pack" is entirely up to you! Your pup's intuitive quest for dominance, coupled with the fact that it is nearly impossible to

Allow your pup to explore, but under your supervision. You never know where he may end up if left to his own devices.

look at an irresistible fluff-ball puppy and not cave in, give the Japanese Spitz a most unfair advantage in getting the upper hand!

A pup will definitely test the waters to see what he can and cannot do. Do not give in to those pleading, dark eyes—stand your ground when it comes to disciplining the pup and make sure that all family members do the same. It will only confuse the pup if Mother tells him to get off the sofa when he is used to sitting up there with Father to watch the nightly news. Avoid discrepancies by having all members of the

to wait until the pup's bad behavior becomes the adult dog's bad habit.

NIPPING

As puppies start to teethe, they feel the need to sink their teeth into anything available...unfortunately, that usually includes your

Eight-week-olds just brimming with personality. The puppy "pack" is where the early life lessons are learned.

household decide on the rules before the pup even comes home...and be consistent in enforcing them! Early training shapes the dog's personality, so you cannot be unclear in what you expect.

COMMON PUPPY PROBLEMS

The best way to prevent puppy problems is to be proactive in stopping an undesirable behavior as soon as it starts. The old saying "You can't teach an old dog new tricks" does not necessarily hold true, but it *is* true that it is much easier to discourage bad behavior in a young developing pup than

DEALING WITH PROBLEMS

The majority of problems that are commonly seen in young pups will disappear as your dog gets older. However, how you deal with problems when he is young will determine how he reacts to discipline as an adult dog. It is important to establish who is boss (ideally it will be you!) right away when you are first bonding with your dog. This bond will set the tone for the rest of your life together.

Your Japanese Spitz will certainly sink his teeth into whatever he finds around the yard...

fingers, arms, hair and toes. You may find this behavior cute for the first five seconds...until you feel just how sharp those puppy teeth are. Nipping is something you want to discourage immediately and consistently with a firm "No!" (or whatever number of firm "Nos" it takes for him to understand that you mean business). Then, replace your finger with an appropriate chew toy. While this behavior is merely annoying when the dog is young, it can become dangerous as your Japanese Spitz's adult teeth grow in and his jaws develop, and he continues to think it is okay to nip at and nibble on his human

friends. Your Japanese Spitz does not mean any harm with a friendly nip, but he also does not know that a friendly nip is not so friendly!

CRYING/WHINING

Your pup will often cry, whine, whimper, howl or make some type of commotion when he is left alone. This is basically his way of calling out for attention to make sure that you know he is there and that you have not forgotten about him. Your puppy feels insecure when he is left alone, when you are out of the house and he is in his crate or when you are in another part of the house and he cannot see you. The noise he is making is an expression of the anxiety he feels at being alone, so he needs to be taught that being alone is okay. You are not actually training the dog to stop making noise; rather, you are training him to feel comfortable when he is alone and thus removing the need for him to make the noise.

This is where the crate with cozy bedding and a toy comes in handy. You want to know that your pup is safe when you are not there to supervise, and you know that he will be safe in his crate rather than roaming freely about the house. In order for the pup to stay in his crate without making a fuss, he first needs to be comfortable in his crate. On that note, it is extremely important that the crate is never used as a form of punishment; this will cause the pup to view the crate as a negative place, rather than as a place of his own for safety and retreat.

Accustom the pup to the crate in short, gradually increasing time intervals in which you put him in the crate, maybe with a treat, and stay in the room with him. If he cries or makes a fuss, do not go to him, but stay in his sight. Gradually he will realize that staying in his crate is just fine without your help, and it will not be so traumatic for him when you are not around. You may want to leave the radio on softly when you leave the house; the sound of human voices may be comforting to him.

...but wouldn't you rather he played with safe dog toys?

FEEDING THE JAPANESE SPITZ

You have arrived home with your new nine-week-old Japanese Spitz puppy. Hopefully you will have asked and received from the breeder a diet sheet along with the rest of the puppy's papers. This will inform you how your puppy has been fed. You should continue with this diet for the next few days, as this will help to avoid digestive upsets. You can then gradually introduce a new type of food if you wish. Start by mixing a little of the new food with the breeder's diet. Be sure to

Offer a food that provides complete and balanced nutrition for small-breed dogs. Your Japanese Spitz's diet figures largely into his overall health and condition.

> **STORING DOG FOOD**
> You must store your dry dog food carefully. Open packages of dog food quickly lose their vitamin value, usually within 90 days of being opened. Mold spores and vermin could also contaminate the food.

introduce only one new food at a time; again, gradual is the key.

Today, it would seem that most breeders recommend a dry kibble. Check the label to make sure that the food you offer your puppy is a "complete food," meaning that it contains all of the necessary vitamins, minerals and protein that are required for a dog of his age. Others prefer a small mixer biscuit and canned puppy food. At this age, your Japanese Spitz puppy should be having four meals a day. I prefer to give breakfast, which should be a cereal-type food mixed with diluted evaporated (not cow's) milk (one part milk to three parts water); then a midday meal of puppy meal and fresh cooked meat or canned puppy food; repeat this for the early evening meal; then before bedtime repeat the meal that you fed at breakfast.

Remember at all times while your puppy is awake and active, he should have access to fresh clean water. You will also find that your puppy will enjoy fresh vegetables, which can be mixed into meals or used as treats, as can fresh fruit (no grapes or raisins!). Most Japanese Spitzen seem to have a great liking for fruit. Remember that how your puppy grows depends a great deal on what he is fed during his

These one-week-old puppies are getting the best start in life by nursing from their mother.

FOOD PREFERENCE

Selecting the best dry dog food is difficult. There is no majority consensus among veterinary scientists as to the value of nutrient analysis (protein, fat, fiber, moisture, ash, cholesterol, minerals, etc.). All agree that feeding trials are what matter most, but you also have to consider the individual dog. The dog's weight, age and activity level, and what pleases his taste, all must be considered. It is probably best to take the advice of your veterinarian. Every dog has individual dietary requirements, and should be fed accordingly.

If your dog is fed a good dry food, he does not require supplements of meat or vegetables. Dogs do appreciate a little variety in their diets, so you may choose to stay with the same brand but vary the flavor. Alternatively, you may wish to add a little flavored stock to give a difference to the taste.

puppy months. At 16 weeks of age, you can cut out one of the milk meals; at 8 months, you can reduce the meals to morning and evening, one milky and one meat. Some owners prefer to keep their dogs on two meals a day, but most reduce feedings to one daily meal by the time they are 15 months old, either morning or evening.

Your Japanese Spitz should be fed a puppy diet until he is 12 months of age, when he should be given a junior food. At 18 months of age, he can be put on an adult-maintenance diet.

You should choose whether or not to put your Japanese Spitz on a dry kibble diet or to use a canned food, or a combination of both. Once on his adult diet, he can usually remain on this diet right through his life. It is recommended not to give a high-protein diet at any time; 18% protein is quite sufficient for Japanese Spitzen, as any higher

> ### GRAIN-BASED DIETS
> Some less expensive dog foods are based on grains and other plant proteins. While these products may appear to be attractively priced, many breeders prefer a diet based on animal proteins and believe that they are more conducive to your dog's health. Many grain-based diets rely on soy protein, which may cause flatulence (passing gas).
>
> There are many cases, however, when your dog might require a special diet. These special requirements should only be recommended by your veterinarian.

sometimes causes skin problems.

The author has not found it necessary to change his dogs to a senior diet, so this switch does not need to be made unless your vet recommends doing so. Depending on your individual dog

and his activity level and health, a senior diet may or may not be warranted.

If you wish to give your dog special treats, use dog biscuits or chews, perhaps two or three a day, but no more. These treats will also help to keep your dog's teeth clean and free of tartar. Avoid tossing "people food" treats to your dog. These can be fattening and cause stomach upset; some foods (like chocolate, onions, nuts, grapes and raisins) are poisonous to dogs.

If you are going to breed your bitch, you will need to increase her food intake when she is about five weeks in whelp. You will need to increase not only the quantity of food but also the quality of her food. Foods that are higher in protein with plenty of calcium (for bone development) are recommended. Some breeders like to give a vitamin and mineral supplement, but be careful not to overdo supplementation, which can cause more problems.

EXERCISE FOR YOUR DOG
The Japanese Spitz is an active breed that thrives on time spent with his owner, preferably outside where he can enjoy the fresh air, sunshine and all the smells of the great outdoors! By and large, the breed does not require a great deal of exercise. Japanese Spitzen are quite happy to go out with their owners on walks or even jogs.

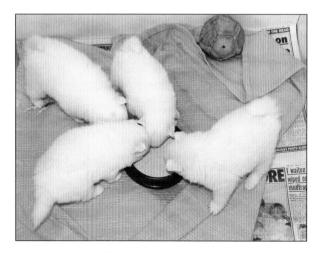

Dinnertime for the litter! Milk and meat meals are introduced to the puppies as part of the weaning process.

A Worthy Investment

Veterinary studies have proven that a balanced high-quality diet pays off in your dog's coat quality, behavior and activity level. Invest in premium brands for the maximum payoff with your dog.

"DOES THIS COLLAR MAKE ME LOOK FAT?"

While humans may obsess about how they look and how trim their bodies are, many people believe that extra weight on their dogs is a good thing. The truth is, pets should not be over- or under-weight, as both can lead to or signal sickness. In order to tell how fit your pet is, run your hands over his ribs. Are his ribs buried under a layer of fat or are they sticking out considerably? If your pet is within his normal weight range, you should be able to feel the ribs easily, but they should not protrude abnormally. If you stand above him, the outline of his body should resemble an hourglass. Some breeds do tend to be leaner while some are a bit stockier, but making sure your dog is the right weight for his breed will certainly contribute to his good health.

Consult your breeder and vet to advise you about the best diet for your Japanese Spitz at the different stages of his life and when to make dietary changes.

They have a surprising amount of stamina. They walk well on-lead and also enjoy "free" running, provided you have a safely enclosed place to allow them off-lead. Never let your Japanese Spitz off-lead when in an unfenced area. Like all other spitz dogs, Japanese Spitzen love to run—and they will keep going until they find Tokyo! They like to chase balls and other objects and will learn to retrieve with very little training.

Japanese Spitzen are equally happy to go out in the yard and run or take a short walk on a lead. They seem able to adapt to their owners' wishes with no ill effect, making them ideally suited for elderly people or city living.

Puppies should not be over-exercised, as this can cause them more harm than good. You can start exercising your puppy with short amounts of road walking each day when he is about 14 weeks of age. Walking on pavement will keep nails short and build up his muscles. The rest of the pup's exercise can be just his normal running around at home and playtime with you. Do not encourage a young puppy to jump, as this can aggravate knee problems, which are not uncommon in the breed.

Japanese Spitzen seem to be very much at home in wooded areas, but some are equally at home in water. Be careful that the

FREE AT LAST!

While running off leash may be great fun for your dog, it can turn into a time when your dog shows you everything you did wrong in obedience class. If you want to give your dog a chance to have some fun and exercise without the constraints of a leash, the best place to do this is in a designated fenced-in area where dogs can socialize and work off excess energy. When visiting such an area, don't let your dog run amok or unattended, watch other dogs that are present and follow all rules, specifically those regarding waste disposal.

GROOMING AND COAT CARE

Of course, the crowning glory of this beautiful breed is his long coat, a feature that requires considerable attention from his doting owner! The Japanese Spitz's long coat consists of a profuse, short, dense, soft-textured undercoat and a straight, stand-off, long outer coat. The Japanese Spitz coat is pure white, which, understandably, can be "off-putting" to some people. Fear not! With a little grooming once a day and a good thorough grooming once a week, your Japanese Spitz will remain sparkling white and covered with a superb coat.

Japanese Spitz males shed their coats once a year; bitches

Jogging partners! If you have more than one dog, they will get a lot of exercise by playing with each other.

dog's coat does not get infested by ticks and other parasites in the great outdoors, or that his swimming holes aren't contaminated by waste or other toxic material.

Japanese Spitzen enjoy agility sports but, again, be careful to not expect too much of them in the way of jumping. Training should not begin until 12 months old. As the dog matures, build up the scope and height of the obstacles on the course gradually. Having offered this warning about jumping, it must be admitted that most Japanese Spitzen enjoy jumping, which makes your role a bit more challenging. It is not at all unusual for a Japanese Spitz to clear a 4-foot-high fence!

DRINK, DRANK, DRUNK—MAKE IT A DOUBLE

In both humans and dogs, as well as other living organisms, water forms the major part of nearly every body tissue. Naturally, we take water for granted but, without it, life as we know it would cease.

For dogs, water is needed to keep their bodies functioning biochemically. Additionally, water is needed to replace the water lost while panting. Unlike humans, who are able to sweat to dissipate heat, dogs must pant to cool down, thereby losing the vital water that their bodies need to regulate their body temperatures. Humans lose electrolyte-containing products and other body-fluid components through sweating; dogs do not lose anything except water. Water is essential always, but especially so when the weather is hot or humid or when your dog is exercising or working vigorously.

twice a year. Once the dog (or bitch) starts to drop coat—you will know it from the clouds of white rolling around your floors—you must brush the dog at least twice a day. Brushing and combing assists the coat in its changeover, removing all the loose dead hair and making way for the fabulous new coat to come in.

If your dog has gotten muddy when out for a walk, do not try to rub it off when you get home; instead, allow the dog to dry off naturally. Once he is dry, you can give the coat a thorough brushing and you will find that the dirt just falls right out, leaving the coat sparkling white again.

For normal grooming, you will need a wide-toothed comb and a fine-toothed comb. You will also find a revolving-tooth comb extremely useful in releasing hair that has formed into a knot without pulling on the hair. Your list of grooming tools should also include a slicker brush and a pin brush, which has the pin ends covered, nail clippers, a nail file, a good-quality pair of pointed-end scissors and a toothbrush and toothpaste made for canines.

For bathing the dog, you require a good-quality shampoo and conditioner, a bath mat (to stop the dog from slipping), several towels and an electric hair dryer. If you can afford a grooming table, you will find that it is an excellent investment. It must have a non-slip surface as well as an arm and "noose" to hold the dog's head during grooming sessions. Although many groomers do without the special tables, those who use them consider them essential, giving them better control of their dogs and sparing their backs from bending over the dogs.

You should not bathe your Japanese Spitz too often, as it removes the oils from the hair. Show people like to bathe before each show, but pet owners should only bathe about four times a year. Do not bathe while your dog is shedding coat, because wetting the coat will just cause the hair to form one large knot, which will take hours to untangle and cause great discomfort to the dog. Once the coat is nearly done shedding, give the dog a good warm bath, and he'll be ready for his new coat.

Now that you have the equipment, it's time to start grooming. Starting at the base of the tail and, working towards the head, use the wide-toothed comb in one hand while the other hand parts the hair and holds the skin down (to avoid any tugging that will hurt the dog). You want to make grooming a pleasant experience for the dog, or else he'll be put off the process and run every time he sees you brandishing your

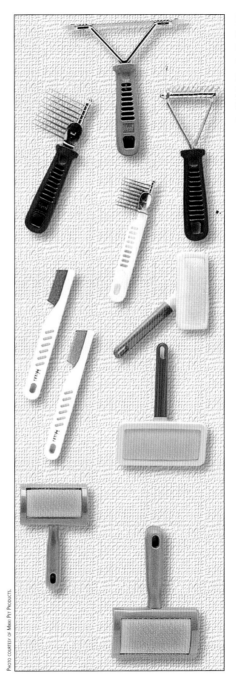

Purchase good-quality grooming tools that will withstand frequent use on your Japanese Spitz's abundant coat.

Gentle strokes with a soft brush will help accustom your puppy to grooming. Even as a youngster, the Japanese Spitz carries a good amount of coat that must be kept mat-free.

comb. For the hair around and under the ears, you will also use the fine-toothed comb. The mane or ruff, which is the hair framing the head around the neck and shoulders, needs to be combed forward, and the hair on the chest needs to be combed outward.

When you are sure that every hair has been combed and all knots removed, the coat should be brushed well. Again start at the base of the tail and work toward the head. Finally, very gently, smooth over the coat with the brush.

Now, having dealt with brushing and combing, let's discuss trimming. There is very little trimming done to the Japanese Spitz; in fact, the only trimming is done to the hair on the back of the back legs as far as the hocks, any straggly hairs on the tops of the toes and the hair that grows between the pads and toes. Trim these areas with the pointed-end scissors.

The nails now need attention. If they have grown long, clip them back, making sure you do not cut back into the "quick." Since the Japanese Spitz has nice dark nails, the quick is not visible and it is quite easy to cut into this vein by accident. Only cut a little at a time—err on the side of caution. Once the nails are cut, smooth them off with the file.

Now it is time to clean your dog's teeth! Remove any tartar

slicker brush!

Comb the hair on the body, starting at the roots and working towards the tips. The longer hair on the stomach should be combed outward and down; the hair on the hindquarters needs to be combed carefully outward. The long hair on the back of the front and back legs should be combed outward. For this finer hair, use the fine-toothed comb; the same goes for the hair on the inside of the back legs. Be careful with the tender skin on the inside of the back legs. The hair on the tail should be combed outward, working from the base towards the tip, using the fine-toothed

A slicker brush can be used over the whole body.

Trimming excess hair gives the feet a neat appearance and shape.

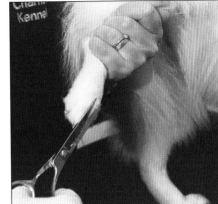

Pay special and gentle attention to the "trousers," the longer hair on the thighs, as these areas are more prone to matting.

The backs of the legs are typically trimmed from hock to foot.

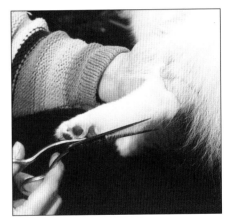

Don't forget the tail! Brush out the long feathering, taking care not to pull or tug and thus cause the dog pain.

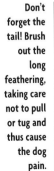

A look at before and after: Trimmed (left) and untrimmed (right).

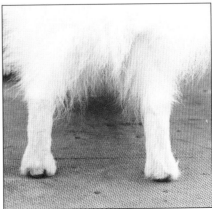

Part of grooming is keeping your dog's ears clean. Use an ear-cleaning powder or liquid, with a soft wipe, cleaning gently and never entering the ear canal.

The area around the eyes also should be kept clean with a damp cloth or specially formulated cleanser to remove tear stains or other debris.

Dogs benefit from having their teeth brushed regularly, and canine-formulated dental-care products are available. Try to brush your Japanese Spitz's teeth at least once a week.

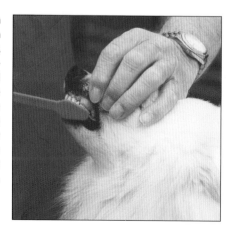

Nail Clipping

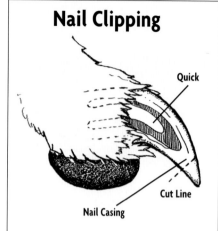

Quick

Cut Line

Nail Casing

DARK-COLORED NAIL

With black or dark nails, it's best to clip only a small bit of the nail at a time or to use a file where the quick is not visible.

LIGHT-COLORED NAIL

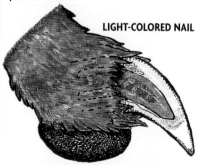

In light-colored nails, clipping is much simpler because you can see the vein (or quick) that grows inside the nail casing.

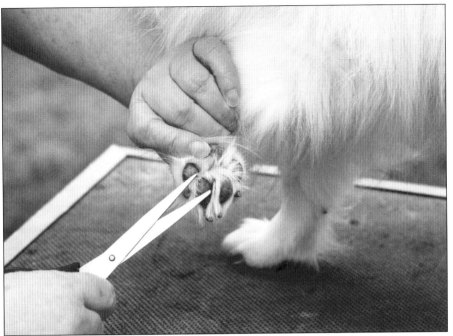

Trimming the excess hair from the bottoms of the feet, between the foot pads, prevents uncomfortable mats from forming.

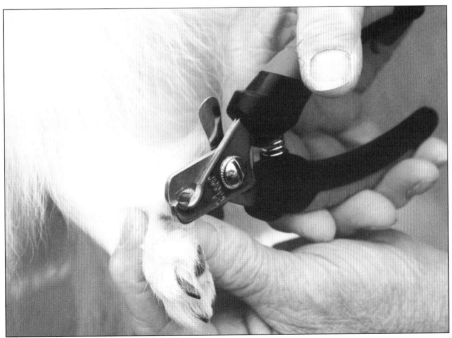

With a careful touch, use nail clippers made for dogs to keep your Japanese Spitz's nails at the proper length.

that has formed, and give a good brushing with the doggy toothbrush and toothpaste. You will find that your dog soon gets used to this procedure and even enjoys the taste of the toothpaste, which comes in flavors appealing to dogs. Never use human toothpaste with your dog.

For certain, the Japanese Spitz is an attractive, lovely breed, and his beauty only requires a small commitment on the part of his owners. After his salon appointment with his beautician—you—let your Japanese Spitz have a good shake. Behold, you have a beautiful dog in pristine, sparkling condition!

TRAVELING WITH YOUR DOG

CAR TRAVEL

You should accustom your Japanese Spitz to riding in a car at an early age. You may or may not take him in the car often, but at the very least he will need to go to

All dressed up with somewhere to go! Your Japanese Spitz might just take the driver's seat if you allow it, but that's not the best bet for safe travel.

> **MOTION SICKNESS**
>
> *If life is a motorway...*your dog may not want to come along for the ride! Some dogs experience motion sickness in cars that leads to excessive salivation and even vomiting. In most cases, your dog will fare better in the familiar, safe confines of his crate. To desensitize your dog, try going on several short jaunts before trying a long trip. If your dog experiences distress when riding in the vehicle, drive with him only when absolutely necessary, and do not feed him or give him water before you go.

the vet and you do not want these trips to be traumatic for the dog or troublesome for you. The safest way for a dog to ride in the car is in his crate. If he uses a crate in the house, you can use the same crate for travel.

Put the pup in the crate and see how he reacts. If he seems uneasy, you can have a passenger hold him on his lap while you drive. Another option for car travel is a specially made safety harness for dogs, which straps the dog in much like a seat belt. Do not let the dog roam loose in the vehicle—this is very dangerous! If you should stop short, your dog can be thrown and injured. If the dog starts climbing on you and pestering you while you are driving, you will not be able to concentrate on the road. It is an

Visit some kennels and take personal recommendations when selecting a boarding kennel convenient to your home. Find one that is clean, affordable and small-dog-friendly, with a knowledgeable, caring staff.

unsafe situation for everyone—human and canine.

For long trips, bring along water for the dog and be prepared to stop to let the dog relieve himself, always keeping him on a lead when you make stops. Take with you whatever you need to clean up after him, including some paper towels and perhaps some old rags or bath towels for use should he have a potty accident in the car or suffer from motion sickness.

Remember that no dog should ever be left alone in a car. Temperatures can soar in a matter of minutes and a dog can die of heat exhaustion in less time than you would ever imagine, despite his perfectly insulated coat. Rolling down the windows helps little and is dangerous in that an overheated dog will panic and attempt to escape through the open window, possibly injuring himself.

AIR TRAVEL

Contact your chosen airline before proceeding with travel plans that include your Japanese Spitz. The dog will be required to travel in a fiberglass crate and you should always check in advance with the airline regarding specific requirements for the crate's size, type and labeling, as well as any health certificates needed for the dog. On many airlines, small pets whose crates fall within the specified size limitations are granted "carry-on" status and can accompany their owners in the cabin. This may be possible with a small Japanese Spitz; again, check with the

THE LOST DOG

You have a valuable dog. If the dog is lost or stolen, you would undoubtedly become extremely upset. Likewise, if you encounter a lost dog, notify the police or the local animal shelter.

airline ahead of time.

To help put the dog at ease, make sure he is accustomed to his travel crate and give him one of his favorite toys in the crate. Feed the dog a light meal several hours prior to checking in so that you minimize his need to relieve himself. For long trips, you will have to include food and water bowls, and a portion of food, attached to the crate so that airline employees can tend to the dog between legs of the trip.

Make sure that your Japanese Spitz is properly identified and that your contact information appears on his ID tags and on his crate. If not permitted in the cabin, your Japanese Spitz will travel in a different area of the plane than human passengers, so every rule must be strictly followed to prevent your dog's getting separated from you.

VACATIONS AND BOARDING

So you want to take a family vacation—and you want to include *all* members of the family. You would probably make arrangements for accommodations ahead of time anyway, but this is especially important when traveling with a dog. You do not want to make an overnight stop at the only place around for miles, only to find out that they do not allow dogs. Also, you do not want to reserve a place for your family without confirming that you are traveling with a dog, because, if it is against their policy, you may end up without a place to stay.

Alternatively, if you are traveling and choose not to bring your Japanese Spitz, you will have to make arrangements for him while you are away. Some options are to take him to a neighbor's house to stay while you are gone, to have a trusted neighbor stop by often or stay at your house or to bring your dog to a reputable boarding kennel. If you choose to board him at a kennel, you should visit in advance to see the facilities provided and where the dogs are kept. Are the dogs' areas spacious and kept clean? Talk to some of the employees and observe how they treat the dogs—

> ### BOARDING QUESTIONS
> Will your dog be exercised at least twice a day? How often during the day will the staff keep him company? Does the kennel provide a clean and secure environment? These are some of the questions you should consider when choosing a boarding kennel.
>
> Likewise, if the staff asks you a lot of questions, this is a good sign. They need to know your dog's personality and temperament, health record, special requirements and what commands he has learned. Above all, follow your instincts. If you have a bad feeling about a kennel, even if a friend has recommended it, don't put your dog in the care of that facility.

IDENTIFICATION OPTIONS

As puppies become more and more expensive, especially those puppies of high quality for showing and/or breeding, they have a greater chance of being stolen. The usual collar dog tag is, of course, easily removed. But there are two more permanent techniques that have become widely used for identification.

The puppy microchip implantation involves the injection of a small microchip, about the size of a corn kernel, under the skin of the dog. If your dog shows up at a clinic or shelter, or is offered for resale under less-than-savory circumstances, he can be positively identified by the microchip. The microchip is scanned, and a registry quickly identifies you as the owner.

Tattooing is done on various parts of the dog, from his belly to his ears. The number tattooed can be your telephone number, your dog's registration number or any other number that you can easily memorize. When professional dog thieves see a tattooed dog, they usually lose interest. For the safety of our dogs, no laboratory facility or dog broker will accept a tattooed dog as stock.

Discuss microchipping and tattooing with your veterinarian and breeder. Some vets perform these services on their own premises for a reasonable fee. To ensure that your dog's identification is effective, be certain that the dog is then properly registered with a legitimate national database.

do they spend time with the dogs, play with them, groom them, etc.? Also find out the kennel's policy on vaccinations and what they require. This is for all of the dogs' safety, since there is a greater risk of diseases being passed from dog to dog when dogs are kept together.

IDENTIFICATION

Your Japanese Spitz is your valued companion and friend. That is why you always keep a close eye on him and you have made sure that he cannot escape from the yard or wriggle out of his collar and run away from you.

However, accidents can happen and there may come a time when your dog unexpectedly becomes separated from you. If this unfortunate event should occur, the first thing on your mind will be finding him. Proper identification, including an ID tag and a microchip, will increase the chances of his being returned to you safely and quickly. Tattooing is also done, though has become less common than microchipping. Discuss these options with your vet, and be sure that your dog is properly registered with a legitimate national database if selecting microchipping or tattooing.

TRAINING YOUR

JAPANESE SPITZ

Living with an untrained dog is a lot like owning a piano that you do not know how to play—it is a nice object to look at, but it does not do much more than that to bring you pleasure. Now try taking piano lessons, and suddenly the piano comes alive and brings forth magical sounds and rhythms that set your heart singing and your body swaying.

The same is true with your Japanese Spitz. Any dog is a big responsibility and, if not trained sensibly, may develop unacceptable behavior that annoys you or could even cause family friction.

To train your Japanese Spitz, you may like to enroll in an obedience class. Teach your dog good manners as you learn how and why he behaves the way he does. Find out how to communicate with your dog and how to recognize and understand his communications with you. Suddenly the dog takes on a new role in your life—he is clever, interesting, well behaved and fun to be with. He demonstrates his bond of devotion to you daily. In other words, your Japanese Spitz does wonders for your ego because he constantly reminds you that you are not only his leader, you are his hero!

Those involved with teaching dog obedience and counseling owners about their dogs' behavior have discovered some interesting facts about dog ownership. For example, training dogs when they are puppies results in the highest rate of success in developing well-mannered and well-adjusted adult dogs. Training an older dog, from six months to six years of age, can produce almost equal results, providing that the owner accepts the dog's slower rate of learning capability and is willing to work patiently to help the dog succeed at developing to his fullest potential. Unfortunately, many owners of untrained adult dogs lack the patience factor, so they do not persist until their dogs are successful at learning particular behaviors.

Training a puppy aged 10 to 16 weeks (20 weeks at the most) is like working with a dry sponge in a pool of water. The pup soaks up whatever you show him and constantly looks for more things to do and learn. At this early age, his body is not yet producing

Young puppies will follow their owners anywhere. Take advantage of your pup's attention to you during this time to teach him as much as you can.

hormones, and therein lies the reason for such a high rate of success. Without hormones, he is focused on his owners and not particularly interested in investigating other places, dogs, people, etc. You are his leader: his provider of food, water, shelter and security. He latches onto you and wants to stay close. He will usually follow you from room to room, will not let you out of his sight when you are outdoors with him and will respond in like manner to the people and animals you encounter. If you greet a

---

ATTENTION!

Your dog is actually training you at the same time you are training him. Dogs do things to get attention. They usually repeat whatever succeeds in getting your attention.

friend warmly, he will be happy to greet the person as well. If, however, you are hesitant or anxious about the approach of a stranger, he will respond accordingly to you.

Once the puppy begins to produce hormones, his natural curiosity emerges and he begins to investigate the world around him. It is at this time when you may notice that the untrained dog begins to wander away from you and even ignore your commands to stay close. When this behavior becomes a problem, you have two choices: get rid of the dog or train

Along with your puppy comes normal puppy behavior. Anything at ground level can fall prey to puppy teeth, so create a puppy-proof environment and direct him to proper objects for chewing.

him. It is strongly urged that you choose the latter option.

You usually will be able to find obedience classes within a reasonable distance from your home, but you can also do a lot to train your dog yourself. Sometimes there are classes available, but the tuition is too costly. Whatever the circum-

> ### REAP THE REWARDS
> If you start with a normal, healthy dog and give him time, patience and some carefully executed lessons, you will reap the rewards of that training for the life of the dog. And what a life it will be! The two of you will find immeasurable pleasure in the companionship you have built together with love, respect and understanding.

stances, the solution to training your dog without formal obedience classes lies within the pages of this book.

This chapter is devoted to helping you train your Japanese Spitz at home. If the recommended procedures are followed faithfully, you may expect positive results that will prove rewarding both to you and your dog.

Whether your new charge is a puppy or a mature adult, the methods of teaching and the techniques we use in training basic behaviors are the same. After all, no dog, whether puppy or adult, likes harsh or inhumane methods. All creatures, however, respond favorably to gentle motivational methods and sincere praise and encouragement. Now let us get started.

HOUSE-TRAINING
You can train a puppy to relieve himself wherever you choose, but

THE CLEAN LIFE

By providing sleeping and resting quarters that fit the dog, and offering frequent opportunities to relieve himself outside his quarters, the puppy quickly learns that the outdoors (or the newspaper if you are training him to paper) is the place to go when he needs to urinate or defecate. It also reinforces his innate desire to keep his sleeping quarters clean. This, in turn, helps develop the muscle control that will eventually produce a dog with clean living habits.

this must be somewhere suitable. You should bear in mind from the outset that when your puppy is old enough to go out in public places, any canine deposits must be removed at once. You will always have to carry with you a small plastic bag or "poop-scoop."

Outdoor training includes such surfaces as grass, soil and cement. Indoor training usually means training your dog to newspaper. When deciding on the surface and location that you will want your Japanese Spitz to use, be sure it is going to be permanent. Training your dog to grass and then changing your mind a few months later is extremely difficult for both dog and owner.

Next, choose the command you will use each and every time you want your puppy to void. "Hurry up" and "Let's go" are examples of commands commonly used by dog owners. Get in the habit of giving the puppy your chosen relief command before you take him out. That way, when he becomes an adult, you will be able to determine if he wants to go out when you ask him. A confirmation will be signs of interest, such as wagging his tail, watching you intently, going to the door, etc.

PUPPY'S NEEDS

Your puppy needs to relieve himself after play periods, after each meal, after he has been sleeping and at any time he indicates that he is looking for a place to urinate or defecate. The urinary and intestinal-tract muscles of very young puppies are not fully developed.

A big help in housebreaking is your puppy's nose. Once he uses his chosen relief site, he will use the scent to locate it each time he needs to go.

Japanese Spitzen are friendly dogs, amenable to training and handling by all members of the family.

Thorofore, liko human babies, puppies need to relieve themselves frequently.

Take your puppy out often—every hour for a ten-week-old, for example—and always immediately after sleeping and eating. The older the puppy, the less often he will need to relieve himself. Finally, as a mature healthy adult, he will require only three to five relief trips per day.

HOUSING

Since the types of housing and control you provide for your puppy have a direct relationship on the success of house-training, we consider the various aspects of both before we begin training. Taking a new puppy home and turning him loose in your house

can be compared to turning a child loose in a sports arena and telling the child that the place is all his! The sheer enormity of the place would be too much for him to handle. Instead, offer the puppy clearly defined areas where he can play, sleep, eat and live. A room of the house where the family gathers is the most obvious choice. Puppies are social animals and need to feel a part of the pack right from the start. Hearing your voice, watching you while you are doing things and smelling you nearby are all positive reinforcers that he is now a member of your pack. Usually a family room, the kitchen or a nearby adjoining breakfast area is ideal for providing safety and security for both puppy and owner.

Within the designated room, there should be a smaller area that the puppy can call his own. An alcove, a wire or fiberglass dog crate or a gated corner from which he can view the activities

---

KEEP SMILING

Never train your dog, puppy or adult, when you are angry or in a sour mood. Dogs are very sensitive to human feelings, especially anger, and if your dog senses that you are angry or upset, he will connect your anger with his training and learn to resent or fear his training sessions.

CANINE DEVELOPMENT SCHEDULE

It is important to understand how and at what age a puppy develops into adulthood.
If you are a puppy owner, consult the following Canine Development Schedule to
determine the stage of development your puppy is currently experiencing.
This knowledge will help you as you work with the puppy in the weeks and months ahead.

Period	Age	Characteristics
First to Third	**Birth to Seven Weeks**	Puppy needs food, sleep and warmth, and responds to simple and gentle touching. Needs mother for security and disciplining. Needs littermates for learning and interacting with other dogs. Pup learns to function within a pack and learns pack order of dominance. Begin socializing pup with adults and children for short periods. Pup begins to become aware of his environment.
Fourth	**Eight to Twelve Weeks**	Brain is fully developed. Pup needs socializing with outside world. Remove from mother and littermates. Needs to change from canine pack to human pack. Human dominance necessary. Fear period occurs between 8 and 12 weeks. Avoid fright and pain.
Fifth	**Thirteen to Sixteen Weeks**	Training and formal obedience should begin. Less association with other dogs, more with people, places, situations. Period will pass easily if you remember this is pup's change-to-adolescence time. Be firm and fair. Flight instinct prominent. Permissiveness and over-disciplining can do permanent damage. Praise for good behavior.
Juvenile	**Four to Eight Months**	Another fear period about 7 to 8 months of age. It passes quickly, but be cautious of fright and pain. Sexual maturity reached. Dominant traits established. Dog should understand sit, down, come and stay by now.

Note: These are approximate time frames. Allow for individual differences in puppies.

MEALTIME

Mealtime should be a peaceful time for your Japanese Spitz. Do not put his food and water bowls in a high-traffic area in the house. For example, give him his own little corner of the kitchen where he can eat undisturbed and where he will not be underfoot. Do not allow small children or other family members to disturb the pup when he is eating.

of his new family will be fine. The size of the area or crate is the key factor here. The area must be large enough so that the puppy can lie down and stretch out, as well as stand up, without rubbing his head on the top. At the same time, it must be small enough so that he cannot relieve himself at one end and sleep at the other without coming into contact with his droppings. Dogs are, by nature, clean animals and will not remain close to their relief areas unless forced to do so. In those cases, they then become dirty dogs and usually remain

that way for life.

The dog's designated area should contain clean bedding and a toy. Avoid putting food or water in the dog's crate before he is fully house-trained, as eating and drinking will activate his digestive processes and ultimately defeat your purpose, not to mention make the puppy very uncomfortable if he always has "to go." Once house-training has been achieved reliably, water must always be made available in his area, in a non-spill container.

CONTROL

By control, we mean helping the puppy to create a lifestyle pattern that will be compatible to that of his human pack (you!). Just as we guide little children to learn our way of life, we must show the puppy when it is time to play, eat, sleep, exercise and even entertain himself.

Your puppy should always sleep in his crate. He should also learn that, during times of household confusion and excessive human activity, such as at breakfast when family members are preparing for the day, he can play by himself in relative safety and comfort in his designated area. Each time you leave the puppy alone, he should understand exactly where he is to stay.

Puppies are chewers and cannot tell the difference between

things like lamp and television cords, shoes, table legs, etc. Chewing into a television cord, for example, can be fatal to the puppy, while a shorted wire can start a fire in the house. If the puppy chews on the arm of the chair when he is alone, you will probably discipline him angrily when you get home. Thus, he makes the association that your coming home means he is going to be punished. (He will not remember chewing the chair and is incapable of making the association of the discipline with his naughty deed.) Accustoming the pup to his designated area not only keeps him safe but also avoids his engaging in destructive behaviors when you are not around.

Times of excitement, such as special occasions, family parties, etc., can be fun for the puppy, providing that he can view the activities from the security of his designated area. He is not underfoot and he is not being fed all sorts of tidbits that will probably cause him stomach distress, yet he still feels a part of the fun.

ESTABLISHING A SCHEDULE
A puppy should be taken to his relief area each time he is released from his designated area, after meals, after play sessions and when he first awakens in the morning (at age ten weeks, this

can mean 5 a.m.!). The puppy will indicate that he's ready "to go" by circling or sniffing busily—do not misinterpret these signs. When you first bring your puppy home, a routine of taking him out every hour is necessary. As the puppy grows, he will be able to wait for longer periods of time.

Keep trips to his relief area short. Stay no more than five or six minutes and then return to the house. If he goes during that time, praise him lavishly and take him indoors immediately. If

THINK BEFORE YOU BARK
Dogs are sensitive to their masters' moods and emotions. Use your voice wisely when communicating with your dog. Never raise your voice at your dog unless you are trying to correct him. "Barking" at your dog can become as meaningless as "dogspeak" is to you.

he does not, but he has an accident when you go back indoors, pick him up immediately, say "No! No!" and return to his relief area. Wait a few minutes, then return to the house again. Never hit a puppy or rub his face in urine or excrement when he has a potty accident!

Once indoors, put the puppy in his crate (for control, *not* for punishment) until you have had time to clean up his accident. Then, release him to the family area and watch him more closely than before. Chances are, his

THE SUCCESS METHOD

Success that comes by luck is usually short-lived. Success that comes by well-thought-out proven methods is often more easily achieved and permanent. This is the Success Method. It is designed to give you, the puppy owner, a simple yet proven way to help your puppy develop clean living habits and a feeling of security in his new environment.

6 Steps to Successful Crate Training

1 Tell the puppy "Crate time!" and place him in the crate with a small treat (a piece of cheese or half of a biscuit). Let him stay in the crate for five minutes while you are in the same room. Then release him and praise lavishly. Never release him when he is fussing. Wait until he is quiet before you let him out.

2 Repeat Step 1 several times a day.

3 The next day, place the puppy in the crate as before. Let him stay there for ten minutes. Do this several times.

4 Continue building time in five-minute increments until the puppy stays in his crate for 30 minutes with you in the room. Always take him to his relief area after prolonged periods in his crate.

5 Now go back to Step 1 and let the puppy stay in his crate for five minutes, this time while you are out of the room.

6 Once again, build crate time in five-minute increments with you out of the room. When the puppy will stay willingly in his crate (he may even fall asleep!) for 30 minutes with you out of the room, he will be ready to stay in it for several hours at a time.

HOW MANY TIMES A DAY?

AGE	RELIEF TRIPS
To 14 weeks	10
14–22 weeks	8
22–32 weeks	6
Adulthood	4
(dog stops growing)	

These are estimates, of course, but they are a guide to the *minimum* number of opportunities a dog should have each day to relieve himself.

accident was a result of your not picking up his signal or waiting too long before offering him the opportunity to relieve himself. Never hold a grudge against the puppy for accidents.

Let the puppy learn that going outdoors means it is time to relieve himself, not to play. Once trained, he will be able to play indoors and out and still differentiate between the times for play versus the times for relief. Help him develop regular hours for naps, being alone, playing by himself and just resting, all in his crate. Encourage him to entertain himself while you are busy with your activities. Let him learn that having you near is comforting, but it is not your main purpose in life to provide him with undivided attention. Each time you put your puppy in his own area, use the same command,

whatever suits best. Soon he will run to his crate or special area when he hears you say those words.

Crate training provides safety for you, the puppy and the home. It also provides the puppy with a feeling of security, and that helps him achieve self-confidence and clean habits. Remember that one of the primary ingredients in house-training your puppy is control. Regardless of your lifestyle, there will always be occasions when you will need to have a place where your dog can stay and be happy and safe. Crate training is the answer for now and in the future.

A bright 12-week-old student, learning the potty routine. If house-training him in your fenced yard, you should lead him to the chosen spot on his leash until he knows his area reliably before letting him off-lead to find it on his own.

TAKE THE LEAD
Do not carry your dog to his relief area. Lead him there on a leash or, better yet, encourage him to follow you to the spot. If you start carrying him to his spot, you might end up doing this routine forever and your dog will have the satisfaction of having trained *you*.

In conclusion, a few key elements are really all you need for a successful house-training method—consistency, frequency, praise, control and supervision. By following these procedures with a normal, healthy puppy, you and the puppy will soon be past the stage of "accidents" and ready to move on to a full and rewarding life together.

ROLES OF DISCIPLINE, REWARD AND PUNISHMENT

Discipline, training one to act in accordance with rules, brings order to life. It is as simple as that. Without discipline, particularly in a group society, chaos will reign supreme and the group will eventually perish. Humans and canines are social animals and need some form of discipline in order to function effectively. They must procure food, reproduce to keep their species going and protect their home base and their young. If there were no discipline in the lives of social animals, they would eventually die from starvation and/or predation by other stronger animals. In the case of domestic canines, discipline in their lives is needed in order for them to understand how their pack (you and other family members) functions and how they must act in order to survive.

A large humane society in a highly populated area recently surveyed dog owners regarding their satisfaction with their relationships with their dogs. People who had trained their dogs were 75% more satisfied with their pets than those who had never trained their dogs.

Dr. Edward Thorndike, a world-famous animal psychologist, established *Thorndike's Theory of Learning*, which states that a behavior that results in a pleasant event tends to be repeated. Furthermore, it concludes that a behavior that results in an unpleasant event tends not to be repeated. It is this theory upon which training methods are based today. For example, if you manipulate a dog to perform a specific behavior and reward him for doing it, he is likely to do it again because he enjoyed the end result.

Occasionally, punishment, a penalty inflicted for an offense, is necessary. The best type of punishment often comes from an outside source. For example, a child is told not to touch the oven because he may get burned. He disobeys and touches the oven. In doing so, he receives a burn. From that time on, he respects the heat of the oven and avoids contact with it. Therefore, a behavior that results in an unpleasant event tends not to be repeated.

A good example of a dog's learning the hard way is the dog who chases the house cat. He is told many times to leave the cat alone, yet he persists in teasing

CALM DOWN
Dogs will do anything for your attention. If you reward the dog when he is calm and attentive, you will develop a well-mannered dog. If, on the other hand, you greet your dog excitedly and encourage him to wrestle with you, the dog will greet you the same way and you will have a hyperactive dog on your hands.

the cat. Then, one day, the dog begins chasing the cat but the cat turns and swipes his claws across the dog's face, leaving the dog with a painful gash on his nose. The result is that the dog stops chasing the cat. A behavior that results in an unpleasant event tends not to be repeated.

Never underestimate the power of a treat when it comes to convincing your Japanese Spitz pup that his attention should be on you.

TRAINING EQUIPMENT

COLLAR AND LEASH

For a Japanese Spitz, the collar and leash that you use for training must be one with which you are easily able to work, not too heavy for the dog and perfectly safe.

TREATS

Have a bag of treats on hand; something nutritious and easy to swallow works best. Use a soft treat, a chunk of cheese or a piece of cooked chicken rather than a dry biscuit. By the time the dog has finished chewing a dry treat, he will forget why he is being rewarded in the first place!

Using food rewards will not teach a dog to beg at the table—the only way to teach a dog to beg at the table is to give him food from the table. In training, rewarding the dog with a food treat will help him associate praise and the treats with learning new behaviors that obviously please his owner.

TRAINING BEGINS: ASK THE DOG A QUESTION

In order to teach your dog anything, you must first get his attention. After all, he cannot learn anything if he is looking away from you with his mind on something else.

To get your dog's attention, ask him "School?" and immediately walk over to him and give him a treat as you tell him "Good dog." Wait a minute or two and repeat the routine, this time with a treat in your hand as you approach within a foot of the dog. Do not go directly to him,

---

FEAR AGGRESSION

Pups who are subjected to physical abuse during training commonly end up with behavioral problems as adults. One common result of abuse is fear aggression, in which a dog will lash out, bare his teeth, snarl and finally bite someone by whom he feels threatened. For example, your daughter may be playing with the dog one afternoon. As they play hide-and-seek, she backs the dog into a corner and, as she attempts to tease him playfully, he bites her hand. Examine the cause of this behavior. Did your daughter ever hit the dog? Did someone who resembles your daughter hit or scream at the dog?

Fortunately, fear aggression is relatively easy to correct. Have your daughter engage in only positive activities with the dog, such as feeding, petting and walking. She should not give any corrections or negative feedback. If the dog still growls or cowers away from her, allow someone else to accompany them. After approximately one week, the dog should feel that he can rely on her for many positive things, and he will also be prevented from reacting fearfully towards anyone who might resemble her.

but stop about a foot short of him and hold out the treat as you ask "School?" He will see you approaching with a treat in your hand and most likely begin walking toward you. As you meet, give him the treat and praise again.

The third time, ask the question, have a treat in your hand and walk only a short distance toward the dog so that he must walk almost all the way to you. As he reaches you, give him the treat and praise again.

By this time, the dog will probably be getting the idea that if he pays attention to you, especially when you ask that question, it will pay off in treats

Produce a tasty morsel and watch the whole gang gather 'round. Imagine the dedication and patience required to train a whole "pack" of dogs.

and enjoyable activities for him. In other words, he learns that "school" means doing great things with you that are fun and that result in positive attention for him.

Remember that the dog does not understand your verbal language; he only recognizes sounds. Your question translates to a series of sounds for him, and those sounds become the signal to go to you and pay attention. The dog learns that if he does this, he will get to interact with you plus receive treats and praise.

THE BASIC COMMANDS

TEACHING SIT

Now that you have the dog's attention, attach his leash and hold it in your left hand, and hold a food treat in your right hand. Place your food hand at the dog's nose and let him lick the treat but not take it from you. Say "Sit" and slowly raise your food hand from in front of the dog's

---

SAFETY FIRST

While it may seem that the most important things to your dog are eating, sleeping and chewing the upholstery on your furniture, his first concern is actually safety. The domesticated dogs we keep as companions have the same pack instinct as their ancestors who ran free thousands of years ago. Because of this pack instinct, your dog wants to know that he and his pack are not in danger of being harmed, and that his pack has a strong, capable leader. You must establish yourself as the leader early on in your relationship. That way, your dog will trust that you will take care of him and the pack, and he will accept your commands without question.

READY, SIT, GO!

On your marks, get set: train! Most professional trainers agree that the sit command is the place to start your dog's formal education. Sitting is a natural posture for most dogs and they respond to the sit exercise willingly and readily. For every lesson, begin with the sit command, so that you start out with a successful exercise. Likewise, you should practice the sit command at the end of every lesson as well because you always want to end on a high note.

nose up over his head so that he is looking at the ceiling. As he bends his head upward, he will have to bend his knees to maintain his balance. As he bends his knees, he will assume a sit position. At that point, release the food treat and praise lavishly with comments such as "Good dog! Good sit!" Remember to always praise enthusiastically, because dogs relish verbal praise from their owners and feel so proud of themselves whenever they accomplish a behavior.

As a sidebar, you will not use food forever in getting the dog to obey your commands. Food is only used to teach new behaviors and, once the dog knows what you want when you give a specific command, you will wean him off the food treats but still maintain the verbal praise. After all, you will always have your voice with you, and there will be many times when you have no food rewards but expect the dog to obey.

TEACHING DOWN

Teaching the down exercise is easy when you understand how the dog perceives the down position, and it is very difficult when you do not. Dogs perceive the down position as a submissive one; therefore, teaching the down exercise by using a forceful method can sometimes make the dog develop such a fear of the down that he either runs away when you say "Down" or he attempts to snap at the person who tries to force him down.

Have the dog sit close alongside your left leg, facing in the same direction as you are. Hold the leash in your left hand and a food treat in your right. Now place your left hand lightly on the top of the dog's shoulders where they meet above the spinal cord. Do not push down on the dog's shoulders; simply rest your left hand there so you can guide the dog to lie down close to your left leg rather than to swing away from your side when he drops.

Now place the food hand at the dog's nose, say "Down" very softly (almost a whisper) and slowly lower the food hand to the dog's front feet. When the food hand reaches the floor, begin moving it forward along the floor in front of the dog. Keep talking softly to the dog, saying things like, "Do you want this treat? You can do this, good dog." Your reassuring tone of voice will help calm the dog as he tries to follow the food hand to get the treat.

When the dog's elbows touch the floor, release the food and praise softly. Try to get the dog to maintain that down position for several seconds before you let him sit up again. The goal here is to get the dog to settle down and not feel threatened in the down position.

TEACHING STAY

It is easy to teach the dog to stay in either a sit or a down position. Again, we use food and praise during the teaching process as we help the dog to understand exactly what it is that we are

DOUBLE JEOPARDY

A dog in jeopardy never lies down. He stays alert on his feet because instinct tells him that he may have to run away or fight for his survival. Therefore, if a dog feels threatened or anxious, he will not lie down. Consequently, it is important to keep the dog calm and relaxed as he learns the down exercise.

CONSISTENCY PAYS OFF

Dogs need consistency in their feeding schedule, exercise and relief visits, and in the verbal commands you use. If you use "Stay" on Monday and "Stay here, please" on Tuesday, you will confuse your dog. Don't demand perfect behavior during training sessions and then let him have the run of the house the rest of the day. Above all, lavish praise on your pet consistently every time he does something right. The more he feels he is pleasing you, the more willing he will be to learn.

expecting him to do.

To teach the sit/stay, start with the dog sitting on your left side as before and hold the leash in your left hand. Have a food treat in your right hand and place your food hand at the dog's nose. Say "Stay" and step out on your right foot to stand directly in front of the dog, toe to toe, as he licks and nibbles the treat. Be sure to keep his head facing upward to maintain the sit position. Count to five and then swing around to stand next to the dog again with him on your left. As soon as you get back to the original position, release the food and praise lavishly.

To teach the down/stay, do the down as previously described. As soon as the dog lies down, say "Stay" and step out on your right foot just as you did in the sit/stay. Count to five and then return to stand beside the dog with him on your left side. Release the treat and praise as always.

Within a week or ten days, you can begin to add a bit of distance between you and your dog when you leave him. When you do, use your left hand open with the palm facing the dog as a stay signal, much the same as the hand signal a police officer uses to stop traffic at an intersection. Hold the food treat in your right hand as before, but this time the food will not be touching the dog's nose. He will watch the food hand and quickly learn that he is going to get that treat as soon as you return to his side.

When you can stand 3 feet away from your dog for 30 seconds, you can then begin building time and distance in both stays. Eventually, the dog can be expected to remain in the stay position for prolonged periods of time until you return to him or call him to you. Always praise lavishly when he stays.

TEACHING COME

If you make teaching "come" a fun experience, you should never have a student that does not love the game or that fails to come when called. The secret, it seems, is never to teach the word "come."

At times when an owner most wants his dog to come when called, the owner is likely to be upset or anxious and he allows these feelings to come through in the tone of his voice when he calls his dog. Hearing that desperation in his owner's voice, the dog fears the results of going to him and therefore either disobeys outright or runs in the opposite direction. The secret, therefore, is to teach the dog a game and, when you want him to come to you, simply play the game. It is practically a no-fail solution!

To begin, have several members of your family take a few food treats and each go into a different room in the house. Everyone takes turns calling the dog, and each person should celebrate the dog's finding him with a treat and lots of happy praise. When a person calls the dog, he is actually inviting the dog to find him and to get a treat

PLAN TO PLAY

The puppy should also have regular play and exercise sessions when he is with you or a family member. Exercise for a very young puppy can consist of a short walk around the house or yard. Playing can include fetching games with a large ball or a special toy. (All puppies teethe and need soft things upon which to chew.) Remember to restrict play periods to indoors within his living area (the family room, for example) until he is completely house-trained.

as a reward for "winning."

A few turns of the "Where are you?" game and the dog will understand that everyone is playing the game and that each person has a big celebration awaiting the dog's success at locating him or her. Once the dog learns to love the game, simply calling out "Where are you?" will bring him running from wherever he is when he hears that all-important question.

The come command is recognized as one of the most important things to teach a dog, but there are trainers who work with thousands of dogs and never use the actual word "come." Yet these dogs will race to respond to a person who uses the dog's name followed by "Where are you?" For example, a woman has a 12-year-old companion dog who went blind, but who never fails to locate her owner when asked, "Where are you?"

Children, in particular, love

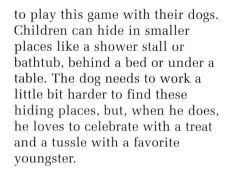

to play this game with their dogs. Children can hide in smaller places like a shower stall or bathtub, behind a bed or under a table. The dog needs to work a little bit harder to find these hiding places, but, when he does, he loves to celebrate with a treat and a tussle with a favorite youngster.

TEACHING HEEL

Heeling means that the dog walks beside the owner without pulling. It takes time and patience on the owner's part to succeed at teaching the dog that he (the owner) will not proceed unless the dog is walking calmly beside him. Neither pulling out ahead on the leash nor lagging behind is acceptable.

Begin by holding the leash in your left hand as the dog sits beside your left leg. Move the loop end of the leash to your right hand, but keep your left hand short on the leash so that it keeps the dog in close next to you.

Say "Heel" and step forward on your left foot. Keep the dog close to you and take three steps. Stop and have the dog sit next to you in what we now call the heel position. Praise verbally, but do not touch the dog. Hesitate a moment and begin again with "Heel," taking three steps and stopping, at which point the dog is told to sit again.

"COME" ... BACK

Never call your dog to come to you for a correction or scold him when he reaches you. That is the quickest way to turn a come command into "Go away fast!" Dogs think only in the present tense, and your dog will connect the scolding with coming to you, not with the misbehavior of a few moments earlier.

You want your Japanese Spitz to come to you eagerly whenever he hears you call him, much like this enthusiastic fellow.

Teach the heel exercise in your fenced yard or another enclosed area, as distraction-free as possible, before expecting him to heel well when out in public among sights and sounds that are sure to capture his interest.

TUG OF WALK?

If you begin teaching the heel by taking long walks and letting the dog pull you along, he misinterprets this action as an acceptable form of taking a walk. When you pull back on the leash to counteract his pulling, he reads that tug as a signal to pull even harder!

Your goal here is to have the dog walk those three steps without pulling on the leash. Once he will walk calmly beside you for three steps without pulling, increase the number of steps you take to five. When he will walk politely beside you while you take five steps, you can increase the length of your walk to ten steps. Keep increasing the length of your stroll until the dog will walk quietly beside you without pulling as long as you want him to heel. When you stop heeling, indicate to the dog that the exercise is over by verbally praising as you pet him and say "OK, good dog." The "OK" is used as a release word, meaning that the exercise is finished and the dog is free to relax.

If you are dealing with a dog who insists on pulling you around, simply "put on your brakes" and stand your ground until the dog realizes that the two of you are not going anywhere until he is beside you and moving at your pace, not his. It may take some time just standing there to convince the dog that you are the leader and that you will be the one to decide on the direction and speed of your travel.

Each time the dog looks up at you or slows down to give a slack leash between the two of you, quietly praise him and say "Good heel. Good dog." Eventually, the dog will begin to respond and within a few days he will be walking politely beside you without pulling on the leash. At first, the training sessions should be kept short and very positive; soon the dog will be able to walk nicely with you for increasingly longer distances. Remember also to give the dog free time and the opportunity to run and play when you have finished heel practice.

WEANING OFF FOOD IN TRAINING

Food is used in training new behaviors. Once the dog understands what behavior goes with a specific command, it is time to start weaning him off the food treats. At first, give a treat after each exercise. Then, start to give a treat only after every other exercise. Mix up the times when you offer a food reward and the times when you offer only praise so that the dog will never know when he is going to receive both

---

HEELING WELL

Teach your dog to heel in an enclosed area. Once you think the dog will obey reliably and you want to attempt advanced obedience exercises such as off-lead heeling, test him in a fenced-in area so he cannot run away.

---

levels of competition include jumping, retrieving, scent discrimination and signal work. The advanced levels require a dog and owner to put a lot of time and effort into their training. The titles that can be earned at these levels of competition are very prestigious.

OTHER ACTIVITIES FOR LIFE

Whether a dog is trained in the structured environment of a class or alone with his owner at home,

Timing is everything when it comes to dispensing rewards. In order to make the connection with the dog, you must praise, treat and/or pet at the moment he performs the intended behavior.

food and praise and when he is going to receive only praise. This is called a variable-ratio reward system. It proves successful because there is always the chance that the owner will produce a treat, so the dog never stops trying for that reward. No matter what, *always* give verbal praise.

OBEDIENCE CLASSES

It is a good idea to enroll in an obedience class if one is available in your area. If yours is a show dog, classes to prepare for the show ring would be more appropriate. Many areas have dog clubs that offer basic obedience training as well as preparatory classes for obedience competition. There are also local dog trainers who offer similar classes.

At obedience trials, dogs can earn titles at various levels of competition, and Japanese Spitzen are very enthusiastic competitors. The beginning levels of obedience competition include basic behaviors such as sit, down, heel, etc. The more advanced

THE STUDENT'S STRESS TEST

During training sessions, you must be able to recognize signs of stress in your dog, such as:

- tucking his tail between his legs
- lowering his head
- shivering or trembling
- standing completely still or running away
- panting and/or salivating
- avoiding eye contact
- flattening his ears back
- urinating submissively
- rolling over and lifting a leg
- grinning or baring teeth
- aggression when restrained

If your four-legged student displays these signs, he may just be nervous or intimidated. The training session may have been too lengthy, with not enough praise and affirmation. Stop for the day and try again tomorrow.

therapy dogs for hospitals and homes for the elderly.

Teaching the dog to help out around the home, in the yard or on the farm provides great satisfaction to both dog and owner. In addition, the dog's help makes life a little easier for his owner and raises his stature as a valued companion to his family. It helps give the dog a purpose by occupying his mind and providing an outlet for his energy. There is little that your Japanese Spitz cannot accomplish if he is trained patiently and consistently. The author knows of one talented Japanese Spitz who enjoys hunting with his owners, picking up downed birds and returning them to the hunters.

If you are interested in participating in organized competition with your Japanese Spitz, there are activities other than obedience in which you and your dog can become involved. Agility is a popular sport in which dogs run through obstacle courses that include various jumps, tunnels and other exercises to test the dog's speed and coordination. Again, as in obedience, the Japanese Spitz tackles agility with great enthusiasm. The owners run beside their dogs to give commands and to guide them through the course. Although competitive, the focus is on fun—it's fun to do, fun to watch and great exercise.

there are many activities that can bring fun and rewards to both owner and dog once they have mastered basic control. Japanese Spitzen are especially adaptive for Hearing Ear programs for the deaf, and they make excellent

A group from Charney Kennels, taking a break during their much-enjoyed agility training.

Conformation showing is competitive while being fun and social, too. Japanese Spitzen love to strut their stuff and they look great doing it.

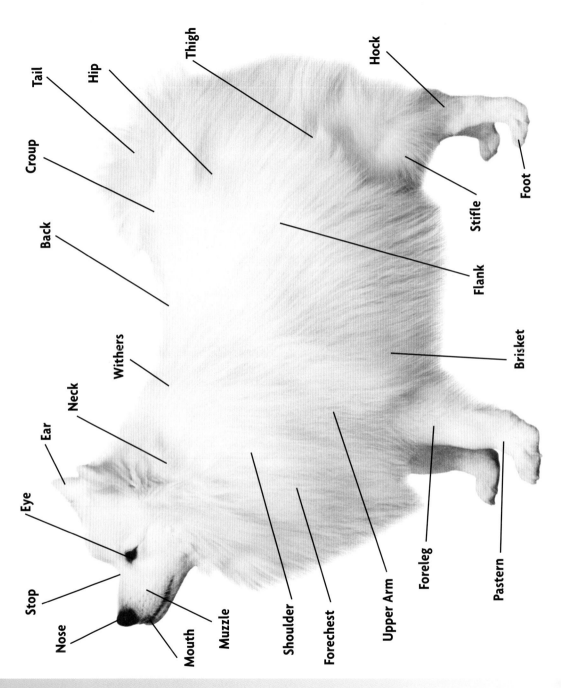

Physical Structure of the Japanese Spitz

HEALTH CARE OF YOUR

JAPANESE SPITZ

Dogs suffer from many of the same physical illnesses as people and might even share many of the same psychological problems. Since people usually know more about human diseases than canine maladies, many of the terms used in this chapter will be familiar but not necessarily those used by veterinarians. For example, we will use the familiar term *x-ray* instead of *radiograph*. We will also use the familiar term *symptoms*, even though dogs don't have symptoms, which are verbal descriptions of something the patient feels or observes himself that he regards as abnormal. Dogs have *clinical signs* since they cannot speak, so we have to look for these clinical signs...but we still use the term *symptoms* in the book.

Medicine is a constantly changing art, of course with scientific input as well. Things alter as we learn more and more about basic sciences such as genetics and biochemistry, and have use of more sophisticated imaging techniques like Computer Aided Tomography (CAT scans) or Magnetic Resonance Imaging (MRI

scans). There is academic dispute about many canine maladies, so different veterinarians treat them in different ways; for example, some vets place a greater emphasis on surgical treatment than others.

SELECTING A QUALIFIED VET
Your selection of a vet should be based on personal recommendation for his skills with dogs, especially small breeds, and, if possible, especially the Japanese Spitz or at least the spitz breeds. If the vet is based nearby, it will be helpful because you might have an emergency or need to make multiple visits for treatments.

All vets are licensed and capable of dealing with routine medical issues such as infections, injuries and the promotion of health (for example, by vaccination and regular exams). If the problem affecting your dog is more complex, your vet will refer your pet to someone with a more detailed knowledge of what is wrong. This will usually be a specialist, perhaps at the nearest university veterinary school, who

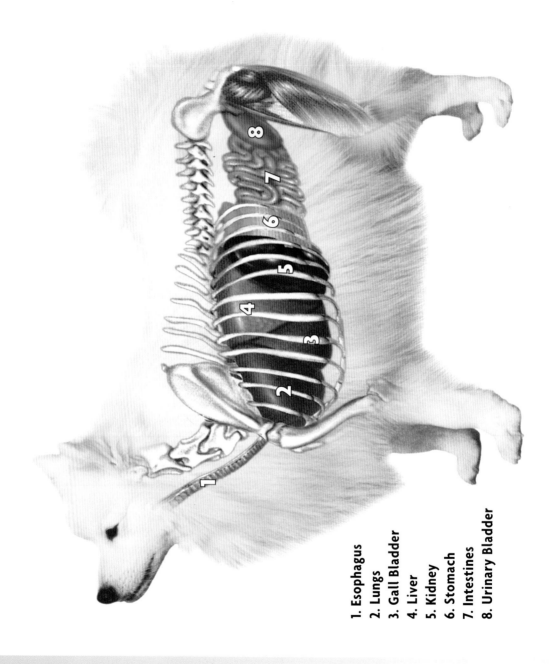

1. Esophagus
2. Lungs
3. Gall Bladder
4. Liver
5. Kidney
6. Stomach
7. Intestines
8. Urinary Bladder

Internal Organs of the Japanese Spitz

concentrates in the field relevant to your dog's problem (e.g., veterinary dermatology, ophthalmology, oncology, etc.).

Veterinary procedures are very costly and, as the treatments available improve, they are going to become more expensive. It is quite acceptable to discuss matters of cost with your vet; if there is more than one treatment option, cost may be a factor in deciding which route to take. It is also acceptable to get a second opinion, but it is courteous to advise the vets concerned that you are doing so.

Insurance against veterinary cost is also becoming very popular. There are a range of policies available. The more extensive policies may cover routine health care, including check-ups, prescription flea prevention and the like.

PREVENTATIVE MEDICINE

It is much easier, less costly and more effective to practice preventative medicine than to fight bouts of illness and disease. Properly bred puppies of all breeds come from parents that were selected based upon their genetic-disease profiles. The puppies' mother should have been vaccinated, free of all internal and external parasites and properly nourished. For these reasons, a visit to the veterinarian who cared for the dam is recommended if at all

Breakdown of Veterinary Income by Category

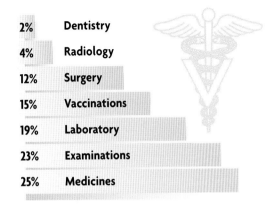

2%	**Dentistry**
4%	**Radiology**
12%	**Surgery**
15%	**Vaccinations**
19%	**Laboratory**
23%	**Examinations**
25%	**Medicines**

possible. The dam passes disease resistance to her puppies, which should last from eight to ten weeks. Unfortunately, she can also pass on parasites and infection. This is why knowledge about her health is useful in learning more about the health of the puppies.

A typical vet's income, categorized according to services performed. This survey dealt with small-animal (pets) practices.

Weaning to Bringing Puppy Home
Puppies should be weaned by the time they are two months old. A puppy that remains for at least eight weeks with his mother and littermates usually adapts better to other dogs and people later in life.

Sometimes new owners have their puppy examined by a veterinarian immediately, which is a good idea unless the puppy is overtired by a long journey home from the breeder. In that case, the appointment should be arranged for the day after bringing the pup home.

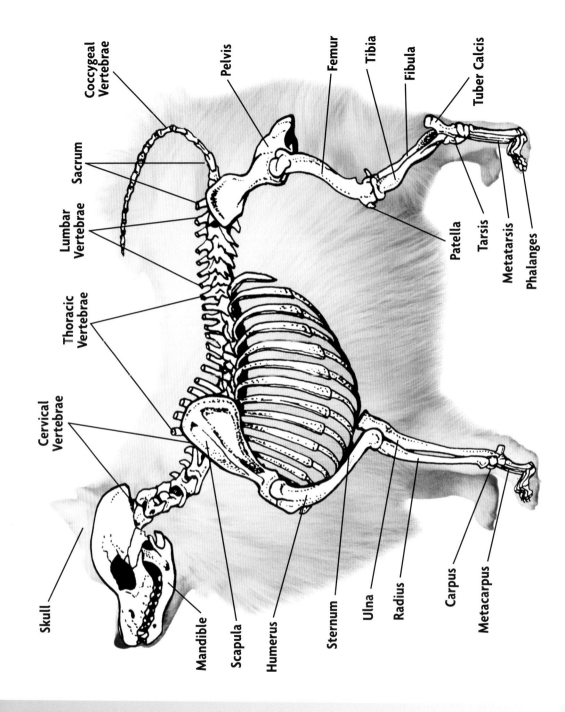

Coccygeal Vertebrae

Pelvis

Femur

Tibia

Fibula

Tuber Calcis

Sacrum

Lumbar Vertebrae

Thoracic Vertebrae

Patella

Tarsis

Metatarsis

Phalanges

Cervical Vertebrae

Skull

Mandible

Scapula

Humerus

Sternum

Ulna

Radius

Carpus

Metacarpus

Skeletal Structure of the Japanese Spitz

The puppy will have his teeth examined and his skeletal conformation and general health checked prior to certification by the vet. Puppies in certain breeds have problems with their kneecaps, cataracts and other eye problems, heart murmurs and undescended testicles. If your vet has training in temperament evaluation, he may be able to evaluate the pup's personality. Also at the first visit, the vet will set up a vaccination schedule.

VACCINATIONS

Most vaccinations are given by injection and should only be given by a vet. Both he and you should keep a record of the date of the injection, the identification of the vaccine and the amount given. Some vets give a first vaccination at six weeks, but most dog breeders prefer the course not to commence until about eight weeks because of the risk of interaction with the antibodies produced by the mother. The vaccination schedule is usually based on a two- to four-week cycle. You must take your veterinarian's advice as to when to vaccinate your puppy, as this may differ according to the type of vaccine used.

HEALTH AND VACCINATION SCHEDULE

AGE IN WEEKS:	6TH	8TH	10TH	12TH	14TH	16TH	20-24TH	52ND
Worm Control	✔	✔	✔	✔	✔	✔	✔	
Neutering							✔	
Heartworm		✔		✔		✔	✔	
Parvovirus	✔		✔		✔		✔	✔
Distemper		✔		✔		✔		✔
Hepatitis		✔		✔		✔		✔
Leptospirosis								✔
Parainfluenza	✔		✔		✔			✔
Dental Examination		✔					✔	✔
Complete Physical		✔					✔	✔
Coronavirus				✔			✔	✔
Canine Cough	✔							
Hip Dysplasia							✔	
Rabies							✔	

Vaccinations are not instantly effective. It takes about two weeks for the dog's immune system to develop antibodies. Most vaccinations require annual booster shots. Your vet should guide you in this regard.

The usual vaccines contain immunizing doses of several different viruses such as distemper, parvovirus, parainfluenza and hepatitis. There are other vaccines available when the puppy is at risk. You should rely upon professional advice. This is especially true for the booster immunizations. Most vaccination programs require a booster when the puppy is a year old and once a year thereafter. In some cases, circumstances may require more or less frequent immunizations.

Canine cough, more formally known as tracheobronchitis, is immunized against with a vaccine that is sprayed into the dog's nostrils. Canine cough is usually included in routine vaccination, but it is often not as effective as the vaccines for other major diseases.

FIVE MONTHS TO ONE YEAR OF AGE
Unless you intend to breed or show your dog, neutering the puppy at the appropriate age is recommended, and is likely required by the breeder if you purchased a pet-quality puppy.

Normal hairs of a dog enlarged 200 times original size. The cuticle (outer covering) is clean and healthy. Unlike human hair that grows from the base, a dog's hair also grows from the end. Damaged hairs and split ends, illustrated above.

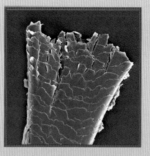
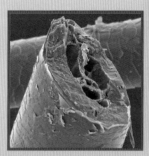

SCANNING ELECTRON MICROGRAPHS BY DR. DENNIS KUNKEL, UNIVERSITY OF HAWAII.

DISEASE REFERENCE CHART

	What is it?	What causes it?	Symptoms
Leptospirosis	Severe disease that affects the internal organs; can be spread to people.	A bacterium, which is often carried by rodents, that enters through mucous membranes and spreads quickly throughout the body.	Range from fever, vomiting and loss of appetite in less severe cases to shock, irreversible kidney damage and possibly death in most severe cases.
Rabies	Potentially deadly virus that infects warm-blooded mammals.	Bite from a carrier of the virus, mainly wild animals.	1st stage: dog exhibits change in behavior, fear. 2nd stage: dog's behavior becomes more aggressive. 3rd stage: loss of coordination, trouble with bodily functions.
Parvovirus	Highly contagious virus, potentially deadly.	Ingestion of the virus, which is usually spread through the feces of infected dogs.	Most common: severe diarrhea. Also vomiting, fatigue, lack of appetite.
Canine cough	Contagious respiratory infection.	Combination of types of bacteria and virus. Most common: *Bordetella bronchiseptica* bacteria and parainfluenza virus.	Chronic cough.
Distemper	Disease primarily affecting respiratory and nervous system.	Virus that is related to the human measles virus.	Mild symptoms such as fever, lack of appetite and mucus secretion progress to evidence of brain damage, "hard pad."
Hepatitis	Virus primarily affecting the liver.	Canine adenovirus type I (CAV-1). Enters system when dog breathes in particles.	Lesser symptoms include listlessness, diarrhea, vomiting. More severe symptoms include "blue-eye" (clumps of virus in eye).
Coronavirus	Virus resulting in digestive problems.	Virus is spread through infected dog's feces.	Stomach upset evidenced by lack of appetite, vomiting, diarrhea.

Discuss all aspects of the procedure with your vet. Neutering and spaying have proven to be extremely beneficial to both male and female puppies, respectively. Besides eliminating the possibility of pregnancy and pyometra in bitches and testicular cancer in male dogs, it greatly reduces the risk of (but does not prevent) breast cancer in bitches and prostate cancer in male dogs.

Your vet should provide your puppy with a thorough dental evaluation at six months of age, ascertaining whether all of the permanent teeth have erupted properly. A home dental-care regimen should be initiated at six months, including brushing weekly and providing good dental devices (such as hard plastic or nylon bones). Regular dental care promotes healthy teeth, fresh breath and a longer life.

DOGS OLDER THAN ONE YEAR
Continue to visit the veterinarian at least once a year. There is no such disease as "old age," but

bodily functions do change with age. The eyes and ears are no longer as efficient. Liver, kidney and intestinal functions often decline. Proper dietary changes, recommended by your veterinarian, can make life more pleasant for your aging Japanese Spitz and you.

SKIN PROBLEMS

Veterinarians are consulted by dog owners for skin problems more than for any other group of diseases or maladies. A dog's skin is as sensitive, if not more so, than human skin, and both can suffer from almost the same ailments (though the occurrence of acne in most breeds is rare). For this reason, veterinary dermatology has developed into a specialty practiced by many vets.

Since many skin problems have visual symptoms that are almost identical, it requires the skill of an experienced veterinary dermatologist to identify and cure many of the more severe skin disorders. Pet shops sell many treatments for skin problems, but most of the treatments are directed at symptoms and not at the underlying problem(s). If your dog is suffering from a skin disorder, you should seek professional assistance as quickly as possible. As with all diseases, the earlier a problem is identified and treated, the more likely it is that the cure will be successful.

HEREDITARY SKIN DISORDERS

Veterinary dermatologists are currently researching a number of skin disorders that are believed to have hereditary bases. These inherited diseases are transmitted by both parents, who appear (phenotypically) normal but have a recessive gene for the disease, meaning that they carry, but are not affected by, the disease. These diseases pose serious problems to breeders because in some instances there are no methods of identifying carriers. Often the secondary diseases associated with these skin conditions are even more debilitating than the skin disorders themselves, including cancers and respiratory problems.

Among the hereditary skin disorders for which the mode of inheritance is known are acrodermatitis, cutaneous asthenia (Ehlers-Danlos syndrome), sebaceous adenitis, cyclic hematopoiesis, dermatomyositis, IgA deficiency, color dilution alopecia and nodular dermatofibrosis. Some of these disorders are limited to one or two breeds, while others affect a large number of breeds. All inherited diseases must be diagnosed and treated by a veterinary specialist.

PARASITE BITES

Many of us are allergic to insect bites. The bites itch, erupt and may even become infected. Dogs have the same reaction to fleas, ticks and/or mites. When an insect lands on you, you have the chance to whisk it away with your hand. Unfortunately, when a dog is bitten by a flea, tick or mite, he can only scratch it away or bite it. By the time the dog has been bitten, the parasite has done some of its damage. It may also have laid eggs, which will cause further problems in the near future. The itching from parasite bites is probably due to the saliva injected into the site when the parasite sucks the dog's blood.

AIRBORNE ALLERGIES

Just as humans suffer from hay fever during the pollinating season, many dogs suffer from the same allergies. When the pollen count is high, your dog might suffer, but don't expect him to sneeze and have a runny nose as a human would. Dogs react to pollen allergies in the same way they react to insect fleas—they scratch and bite themselves. Dogs, like humans, can be tested for allergens. Discuss the testing with your vet.

AUTO-IMMUNE ILLNESSES

An auto-immune illness is one in which the immune system overacts and does not recognize parts of the affected person; rather, the immune system starts to react as if these parts were foreign and need to be destroyed.

An example is rheumatoid arthritis, which occurs when the body does not recognize the joints, thus leading to a very painful and damaging reaction in the joints. This has nothing to do with age, so can occur in children and young dogs. The wear-and-tear arthritis of the older person or dog is osteoarthritis.

Lupus is an auto-immune disease that affects dogs as well as people. It can take variable forms, affecting the kidneys, bones and skin. It can be fatal, so is treated with steroids, which can themselves have very significant side effects. The steroids calm down the allergic reaction to the body's tissues, which helps the

---

A SKUNKY PROBLEM

Have you noticed your dog dragging his rump along the floor? If so, it is likely that his anal sacs are impacted or possibly infected. The anal sacs are small pouches located on both sides of the anus under the skin and muscles. They are about the size and shape of a grape and contain a foul-smelling liquid. Their contents are usually emptied when the dog has a bowel movement but, if not emptied completely, they will impact, which will cause your dog much pain. Fortunately, your veterinarian can tend to this problem easily by draining the sacs for the dog. Be aware that your dog might also empty his anal sacs in cases of extreme fright.

lupus, but the steroids also lessen the body's reaction to real foreign substances such as bacteria as well as thin the skin and bone.

FOOD PROBLEMS

FOOD ALLERGIES

Some dogs can be allergic to many foods that are best-sellers and highly recommended by breeders and vets. Changing the brand of food that you buy may not eliminate the problem if the element to which the dog is allergic is contained in the new brand.

Recognizing a food allergy in a dog can be difficult. Humans often have rashes when they eat foods to which they are allergic, or have swelling of the lips or eyes. Dogs do not usually develop rashes, but react in the same way as they do to an airborne or bite allergy—they itch, scratch and bite. While pollen allergies are usually seasonal, food allergies are year-round problems.

TREATING FOOD ALLERGY

Diagnosis of food allergy is based on a two- to four-week dietary trial with a home-cooked diet fed to the exclusion of all other foods. The diet should consist of boiled rice or potato with a source of protein that the dog has never eaten before, such as fresh or frozen fish, lamb or even something as exotic as pheasant. Water has to be the only drink, and it is really important that no other foods are fed during this trial. If the dog's condition improves, you will need to try the original diet once again to see if the itching resumes. If it does, then this confirms the diagnosis that the dog is allergic to his original diet. The treatment is long-term feeding of something that does not distress the dog's skin, which may be in the form of one of the commercially available hypoallergenic diets or the home-made diet that you created for the allergy trial.

FOOD INTOLERANCE

Food intolerance is the inability of the dog to completely digest certain foods. This occurs because the dog does not have the chemicals necessary to digest some foodstuffs. These chemicals are called enzymes. All puppies have the enzymes necessary to digest canine milk, but some dogs do not have the enzymes to digest a very different form of milk that is commonly found in human households—milk from cows. In such dogs, drinking cows' milk results in loose bowels, stomach pains and the passage of gas.

Dogs often do not have the enzymes to digest soy or other beans. The treatment is to exclude the foodstuffs that upset your Japanese Spitz's digestion.

First Aid at a Glance

Burns
Place the affected area under cool water; use ice if only a small area is burnt.

Bee stings/Insect bites
Apply ice to relieve swelling; antihistamine dosed properly.

Animal bites
Clean any bleeding area; apply pressure until bleeding subsides; go to the vet.

Spider bites
Use cold compress and a pressurized pack to inhibit venom's spreading.

Antifreeze poisoning
Induce vomiting with hydrogen peroxide. Seek *immediate* veterinary help!

Fish hooks
Removal best handled by vet; hook must be cut in order to remove.

Snake bites
Pack ice around bite; contact vet quickly; identify snake for proper antivenin.

Car accident
Move dog from roadway with blanket; seek veterinary aid.

Shock
Calm the dog; keep him warm; seek immediate veterinary help.

Nosebleed
Apply cold compress to the nose; apply pressure to any visible abrasion.

Bleeding
Apply pressure above the area; treat wound by applying a cotton pack.

Heat stroke
Submerge dog in cold bath; cool down with fresh air and water; go to the vet.

Frostbite/Hypothermia
Warm the dog with a warm bath, electric blankets or hot water bottles.

Abrasions
Clean the wound and wash out thoroughly with fresh water; apply antiseptic.

 Remember: an injured dog may attempt to bite a helping hand from fear and confusion. Always muzzle the dog before trying to offer assistance.

A male dog flea, *Ctenocephalides canis.*

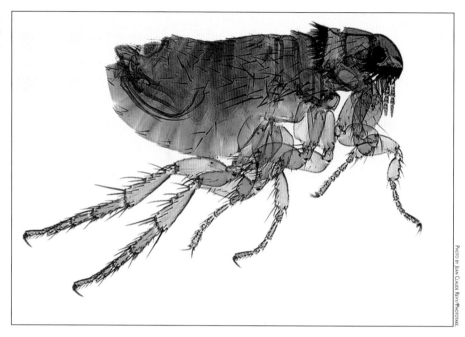

PHOTO BY JEAN CLAUDE REVY-PHOTOTAKE

EXTERNAL PARASITES

FLEAS

Of all the problems to which dogs are prone, none is more well known and frustrating than fleas. Flea infestation is relatively simple to cure but difficult to prevent. Parasites that are harbored inside the body are a bit more difficult to eradicate but they are easier to control.

To control flea infestation, you have to understand the flea's life cycle. Fleas are often thought of as a summertime problem, but centrally heated homes have changed the patterns and fleas can be found at any time of the year. The most effective method of flea control is a two-stage approach: one stage to kill the adult fleas, and the other to control the development of pre-adult fleas. Unfortunately, no single active ingredient is effective against all stages of the life cycle.

FLEA KILLER CAUTION— "POISON"

Flea-killers are poisonous. You should not spray these toxic chemicals on areas of a dog's body that he licks, including his genitals and his face. Flea killers taken internally are a better answer, but check with your vet in case internal therapy is not advised for your dog.

Life Cycle Stages

During its life, a flea will pass through four life stages: egg, larva, pupa or nymph and adult. The adult stage is the most visible and irritating stage of the flea life cycle, and this is why the majority of flea-control products concentrate on this stage. The fact is that adult fleas account for only 1% of the total flea population, and the other 99% exist in pre-adult stages, i.e., eggs, larvae and nymphs. The pre-adult stages are barely visible to the naked eye.

The Life Cycle of the Flea

Eggs are laid on the dog, usually in quantities of about 20 or 30, several times a day. The adult female flea must have a blood meal before each egg-laying session. When first laid, the eggs will cling to the dog's hair, as the eggs are still moist. However, they will quickly dry out and fall from the dog, especially if the dog moves around or scratches. Many eggs will fall off in the dog's favorite area or an area in which he spends a lot of time, such as his bed.

Once the eggs fall from the dog onto the carpet or furniture, they will hatch into larvae. This takes from one to ten days. Larvae are not particularly mobile and will usually travel only a few inches from where they hatch. However, they do have a tendency to move away from bright light and heavy

**EN GARDE:
CATCHING FLEAS OFF GUARD!**
Consider the following ways to arm yourself against fleas:
- Add a small amount of pennyroyal or eucalyptus oil to your dog's bath. These natural remedies repel fleas.
- Supplement your dog's food with fresh garlic (minced or grated) and a hearty amount of brewer's yeast, both of which ward off fleas.
- Use a flea comb on your dog daily. Submerge fleas in a cup of bleach to kill them quickly.
- Confine the dog to only a few rooms to limit the spread of fleas in the home.
- Vacuum daily...and get all of the crevices! Dispose of the bag every few days until the problem is under control.
- Wash your dog's bedding daily. Cover cushions where your dog sleeps with towels, and wash the towels often.

traffic—under furniture and behind doors are common places to find high quantities of flea larvae.

The flea larvae feed on dead organic matter, including adult flea feces, until they are ready to change into adult fleas. Fleas will usually remain as larvae for around seven days. After this period, the larvae will pupate into protective pupae. While inside the pupae, the larvae will undergo metamorphosis and change into

Fleas have been measured as being able to jump 300,000 times and can jump over 150 times their length in any direction, including straight up.

adult fleas. This can take as little time as a few days, but the adult fleas can remain inside the pupae waiting to hatch for up to two years. The pupae are signaled to hatch by certain stimuli, such as physical pressure—the pupae's being stepped on, heat from an animal's lying on the pupae or increased carbon-dioxide levels and vibrations—indicating that a suitable host is available.

Once hatched, the adult flea must feed within a few days. Once the adult flea finds a host, it will not leave voluntarily. It only becomes dislodged by grooming or the host animal's scratching. The adult flea will remain on the

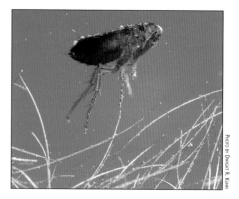

PHOTO BY DWIGHT R. KUHN

host for the duration of its life unless forcibly removed.

TREATING THE ENVIRONMENT AND THE DOG

Treating fleas should be a two-pronged attack. First, the environment needs to be treated; this includes carpets and furniture, especially the dog's bedding and areas underneath furniture. The environment should be treated with a household spray containing an Insect Growth Regulator (IGR) and an insecticide to kill the adult fleas. Most IGRs are effective against eggs and larvae; they actually mimic the fleas' own hormones and stop the eggs and larvae from developing into adult fleas. There are currently no treatments available to attack the pupa stage of the life cycle, so the adult insecticide is used to kill the newly hatched adult fleas before they find a host. Most IGRs are active for many months, while adult insecticides are only active

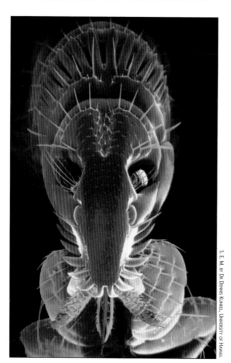

A scanning electron micrograph of a dog or cat flea, *Ctenocephalides*, magnified more than 100x. This image has been colorized for effect.

S. E. M. BY DR. DENNIS KUNKEL, UNIVERSITY OF HAWAII

THE LIFE CYCLE OF THE FLEA

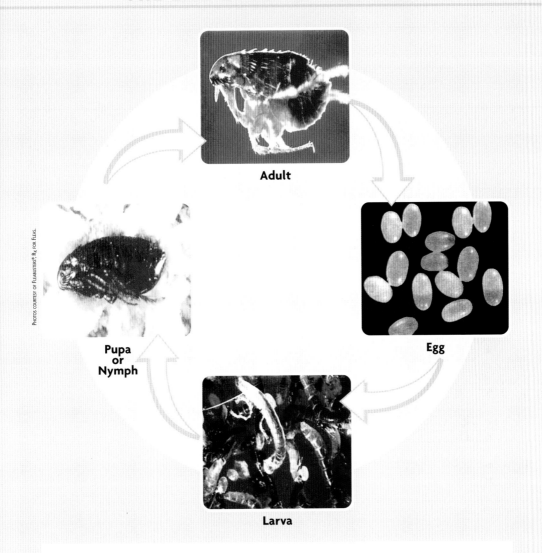

Adult

Egg

Larva

Pupa
or
Nymph

Fleas have been around for millions of years and have adapted to changing host animals. They are able to go through a complete life cycle in less than one month or they can extend their lives to almost two years by remaining as pupae or cocoons. They do not need blood or any other food for up to 20 months.

INSECT GROWTH REGULATOR (IGR)

Two types of products should be used when treating fleas—a product to treat the pet and a product to treat the home. Adult fleas represent less than 1% of the flea population. The pre-adult fleas (eggs, larvae and pupae) represent more than 99% of the flea population and are found in the environment; it is in the case of pre-adult fleas that products containing an Insect Growth Regulator (IGR) should be used in the home.

IGRs are a new class of compounds used to prevent the development of insects. They do not kill the insect outright, but instead use the insect's biology against it to stop it from completing its growth. Products that contain methoprene are the world's first and leading IGRs. Used to control fleas and other insects, this type of IGR will stop flea larvae from developing and protect the house for up to seven months.

The American dog tick, *Dermacentor variabilis*, is probably the most common tick found on dogs. Look at the strength in its eight legs! No wonder it's hard to detach them.

is to apply an adult insecticide to the dog. Traditionally, this would be in the form of a collar or a spray, but more recent innovations include digestible insecticides that poison the fleas when they ingest the dog's blood. Alternatively, there are drops that, when placed on the back of the dog's neck, spread throughout the hair and skin to kill adult fleas.

TICKS

Though not as common as fleas, ticks are found all over the tropical and temperate world. They don't bite, like fleas; they harpoon. They dig their sharp proboscis (nose) into the dog's skin and drink the blood. Their only food and drink is dogs'

for a few days.

When treating with a household spray, it is a good idea to vacuum before applying the product. This stimulates as many pupae as possible to hatch into adult fleas. The vacuum cleaner should also be treated with an insecticide to prevent the eggs and larvae that have been collected in the vacuum bag from hatching.

The second stage of treatment

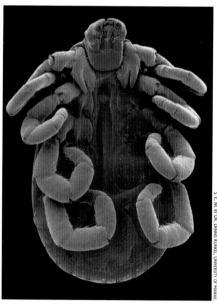

S. E. M. BY DR. DENNIS KUNKEL, UNIVERSITY OF HAWAII

blood. Dogs can get Lyme disease, Rocky Mountain spotted fever, tick bite paralysis and many other diseases from ticks. They may live where fleas are found and they like to hide in cracks or seams in walls. They are controlled the same way fleas are controlled.

The American dog tick, *Dermacentor variabilis*, may well be the most common dog tick in many geographical areas, especially those areas where the climate is hot and humid. Most dog ticks have life expectancies of a week to six months, depending upon climatic conditions. They can neither jump nor fly, but they can crawl slowly and can range up to 16 feet to reach a sleeping or unsuspecting dog.

MITES

Just as fleas and ticks can be problematic for your dog, mites can also lead to an itchy nuisance. Microscopic in size, mites are related to ticks and generally take up permanent residence on their host animal— in this case, your dog! The term *mange* refers to any infestation caused by one of the mighty mites, of which there are six varieties that concern dog owners.

Demodex mites cause a condition known as demodicosis (sometimes called red mange or

DEER-TICK CROSSING

The great outdoors may be fun for your dog, but it also is a home to dangerous ticks. Deer ticks carry a bacterium known as *Borrelia burgdorferi* and are most active in the autumn and spring. When infections are caught early, penicillin and tetracycline are effective antibiotics, but, if left untreated, the bacteria may cause neurological, kidney and cardiac problems as well as long-term trouble with walking and painful joints.

S. E. M. BY DR. ANDREW SPIELMAN/PHOTOTAKE.

PHOTO BY DR. DENNIS KUNKEL, UNIVERSITY OF HAWAII.

The head of an American dog tick, *Dermacentor variabilis*, enlarged and colorized for effect.

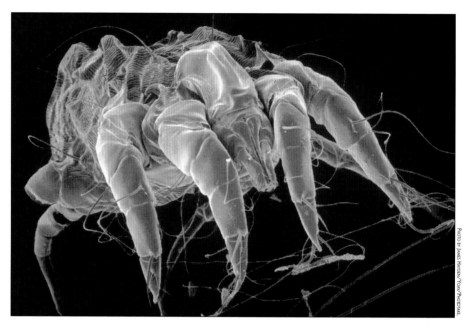

PHOTO BY JAMES HAYDEN/YOAV/PHOTOTAKE

The mange mite, *Psoroptes bovis*, can infest cattle and other domestic animals.

Human lice look like dog lice; the two are closely related.

PHOTO BY DWIGHT R. KUHN.

follicular mange), in which the mites live in the dog's hair follicles and sebaceous glands in larger-than-normal numbers. This type of mange is commonly passed from the dam to her puppies and usually shows up on the puppies' muzzles, though demodicosis is not transferable from one normal dog to another. Most dogs recover from this type of mange without any treatment, though topical therapies are commonly prescribed by the vet.

The *Cheyletiellosis* mite is the hook-mouthed culprit associated with "walking dandruff," a condition that affects dogs as well as cats and rabbits. This mite lives on the surface of the animal's skin and is readily transferable through direct or indirect contact with an affected animal. The dandruff is present in the form of scaly skin, which may or may not be itchy. If not treated, this mange can affect a whole kennel of dogs and can be spread to humans as well.

The *Sarcoptes* mite causes intense itching on the dog in the form of a condition known as scabies or sarcoptic mange. The cycle of the *Sarcoptes* mite lasts about three weeks, and the mites live in the top layer of the dog's skin (epidermis), preferably in areas with little hair. Scabies is highly contagious and can be passed to humans. Sometimes an allergic reaction to the mite worsens the severe itching associated with sarcoptic mange.

Ear mites, *Otodectes cynotis,* lead to otodectic mange, which most commonly affects the outer ear canal of the dog, though other areas can be affected as well. Dogs with ear-mite infestation commonly scratch at their ears, causing further irritation, and shake their heads. Dark-brown droppings in the outer ear confirm the diagnosis. Your vet can prescribe a treatment to flush out the ears and kill any eggs in the ears. A complete month of treatment is necessary to cure the mange.

Two other mites, less common in dogs, include *Dermanyssus gallinae* (the poultry or red mite) and *Eutrombicula alfreddugesi* (the North American mite associated with trombiculidiasis or chigger infestation). The poultry mite frequently lives on chickens, but can transfer to dogs who spend time near farm animals. Chigger infestation affects dogs in the

NOT A DROP TO DRINK
Never allow your dog to swim in polluted water or public areas where water quality can be suspect. Even perfectly clear water can harbor parasites, many of which can cause serious to fatal illnesses in canines. Areas inhabited by waterfowl and other wildlife are especially dangerous.

central US who have exposure to woodlands. The types of mange caused by both of these mites are treatable by vets.

INTERNAL PARASITES
Most animals—fishes, birds and mammals, including dogs and humans—have worms and other parasites that live inside their bodies. According to Dr. Herbert R. Axelrod, the fish pathologist, there are two kinds of parasites: dumb and smart. The smart parasites live in peaceful cooperation with their hosts (symbiosis), while the dumb parasites kill their hosts. Most worm infections are relatively easy to control. If they are not controlled, they weaken the host dog to the point that other medical problems occur, but they do not kill the host as dumb parasites would.

A brown dog tick, *Rhipicephalus sanguineus*, is an uncommon but annoying tick found on dogs.

DO NOT MIX
Never mix parasite-control products without first consulting your vet. Some products can become toxic when combined with others and can cause fatal consequences.

The roundworm *Rhabditis* can infect both dogs and humans.

The roundworm, *Ascaris lumbricoides.*

ROUNDWORMS

Average-size dogs can pass 1,360,000 roundworm eggs every day. For example, if there were only 1 million dogs in the world, the world would be saturated with thousands of tons of dog feces. These feces would contain around 15,000,000,000 roundworm eggs.

Up to 31% of home yards and children's sand boxes in the US contain roundworm eggs.

Flushing dog's feces down the toilet is not a safe practice because the usual sewage treatments do not destroy roundworm eggs.

Infected puppies start shedding roundworm eggs at three weeks of age. They can be infected by their mother's milk.

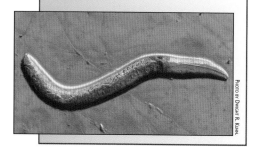

ROUNDWORMS

The roundworms that infect dogs are known scientifically as *Toxocara canis.* They live in the dog's intestines and shed eggs continually. It has been estimated that a dog produces about 6 or more ounces of feces every day. Each ounce of feces averages hundreds of thousands of roundworm eggs. There are no known areas in which dogs roam that do not contain roundworm eggs. The greatest danger of roundworms is that they infect people, too! It is wise to have your dog tested regularly for roundworms.

In young puppies, roundworms cause bloated bellies, diarrhea, coughing and vomiting, and are transmitted from the dam (through blood or milk). Affected puppies will not appear as animated as normal puppies. The worms appear spaghetti-like, measuring as long as 6 inches. Adult dogs can acquire roundworms through coprophagia (eating contaminated feces) or by killing rodents that carry roundworms.

Roundworm infection can kill puppies and cause severe problems in adults, as the hatched larvae travel to the lungs and trachea through the bloodstream. Cleanliness is the best preventative for roundworms. Always pick up after your dog and dispose of feces in appropriate receptacles.

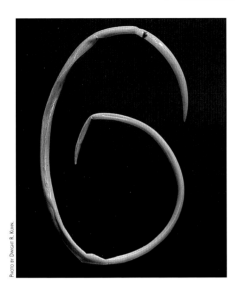

PHOTO BY DWIGHT R. KUHN

HOOKWORMS

In the United States, dog owners have to be concerned about four different species of hookworm, the most common and most serious of which is *Ancylostoma caninum*, which prefers warm climates. The others are *Ancylostoma braziliense*, *Ancylostoma tubaeforme* and *Uncinaria stenocephala*, the latter of which is a concern to dogs living in the northern US and Canada, as this species prefers cold climates.

Hookworms are dangerous to humans as well as to dogs and cats, and can be the cause of severe anemia due to iron deficiency. The worm uses its teeth to attach itself to the dog's intestines and changes the site of its attachment about six times per day. Each time the worm reposi-

tions itself, the dog loses blood and can become anemic. *Ancylostoma caninum* is the most likely of the four species to cause anemia in the dog.

Symptoms of hookworm infection include dark stools, weight loss, general weakness, pale coloration and anemia, as well as possible skin problems. Fortunately, hookworms are easily purged from the affected dog with a number of medications that have proven effective. Discuss these with your vet. Most heartworm preventatives include a hookworm insecticide as well.

Owners also must be aware that hookworms can infect humans, who can acquire the larvae through exposure to contaminated feces. Since the worms cannot complete their life cycle on a human, the worms simply infest the skin and cause irritation. This condition is known as cutaneous larva migrans syndrome. As a preventative, use disposable gloves or a "poop-scoop" to pick up your dog's droppings and prevent your dog (or neighborhood cats) from defecating in children's play areas.

The hookworm, *Ancylostoma caninum*.

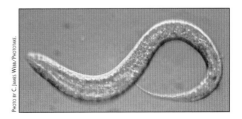

PHOTO BY C. JAMES WEBB/PHOTOTAKE.

The infective stage of the hookworm larva.

TAPEWORMS

Humans, rats, squirrels, foxes, coyotes, wolves and domestic dogs are all susceptible to tapeworm infection. Except in humans, tapeworms are usually not a fatal infection. Infected individuals can harbor 1000 parasitic worms.

Tapeworms, like some other types of worm, are hermaphroditic, meaning male and female in the same worm.

If dogs eat infected rats or mice, or anything else infected with tapeworm, they get the tapeworm disease. One month after attaching to a dog's intestine, the worm starts shedding eggs. These eggs are infective immediately. Infective eggs can live for a few months without a host animal.

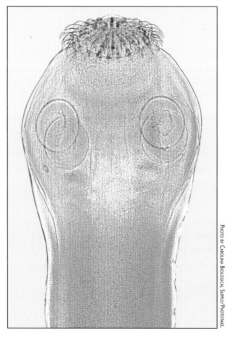

The head and rostellum (the round prominence on the scolex) of a tapeworm, which infects dogs and humans.

PHOTO BY CAROLINA BIOLOGICAL SUPPLY/PHOTOTAKE.

TAPEWORMS

There are many species of tapeworm, all of which are carried by fleas! The most common tapeworm affecting dogs is known as *Dipylidium caninum*. The dog eats the flea and starts the tapeworm cycle. Humans can also be infected with tapeworms—so don't eat fleas! Fleas are so small that your dog could pass them onto your hands, your plate or your food and thus make it possible for you to ingest a flea that is carrying tapeworm eggs.

While tapeworm infection is not life-threatening in dogs (smart parasite!), it can be the cause of a very serious liver disease for humans. About 50% of the humans infected with *Echinococcus multilocularis*, a type of tapeworm that causes alveolar hydatid, perish.

WHIPWORMS

In North America, whipworms are counted among the most common parasitic worms in dogs. The whipworm's scientific name is *Trichuris vulpis*. These worms attach themselves in the lower parts of the intestine, where they feed. Affected dogs may only experience upset tummies, colic and diarrhea. These worms, however, can live for months or years in the dog, beginning their larval stage in the small intestine, spending their adult stage in the large intestine and finally passing infective eggs through the dog's feces. The only way to detect whipworms is through a fecal examination, though this is not always foolproof. Treatment for whipworms is tricky, due to the worms' unusual life-cycle pattern, and very often dogs are reinfected due to exposure to infective eggs on the ground. The whipworm eggs can survive in the environment for as long as five years; thus, cleaning up droppings in your own backyard as well as in public places is absolutely essential for sanitation purposes and the health of your dog and others.

THREADWORMS
Though less common than roundworms, hookworms and those previously mentioned, threadworms concern dog owners in the southwestern US and Gulf Coast area where the climate is hot and humid. Living in the small intestine of the dog, this worm measures a mere 2 millimeters and is round in shape. Like that of the whipworm, the threadworm's life cycle is very complex and the eggs and larvae are passed through the feces. A deadly disease in humans, *Strongyloides* readily infects people, and the handling of feces is the most common means of transmission. Threadworms are most often seen in young puppies; bloody diarrhea and pneumonia are symptoms. Sick puppies must be isolated and treated immediately; vets recommend a follow-up treatment one month later.

HEARTWORM PREVENTATIVES

There are many heartworm preventatives on the market, many of which are sold at your veterinarian's office. These products can be given daily or monthly, depending on the manufacturer's instructions. All of these preventatives contain chemical insecticides directed at killing heartworms, which leads to some controversy among dog owners. In effect, heartworm preventatives are necessary evils, though you should determine how necessary based on your pet's lifestyle. There is no doubt that heartworm is a dreadful disease that threatens the lives of dogs. However, the likelihood of your dog's being bitten by an infected mosquito is slim in most places, and a mosquito-repellent (or an herbal remedy such as Wormwood or Black Walnut) is much safer for your dog and will not compromise his immune system (the way heartworm preventatives will). Should you decide to use the traditional preventative "medications," you can consider giving the pill every other or third month. Since the toxins in the pill will kill the heartworms at all stages of development, the pill would be effective in killing larvae, nymphs or adults, and it takes four months for the larvae to reach the adult stage. Thus, there is no rationale to poisoning the dog's system on a monthly basis. Lastly, do not give the pill during the winter months since there are no mosquitoes around to pass on their infection, unless you live in a tropical environment.

Life Cycle of the Heartworm

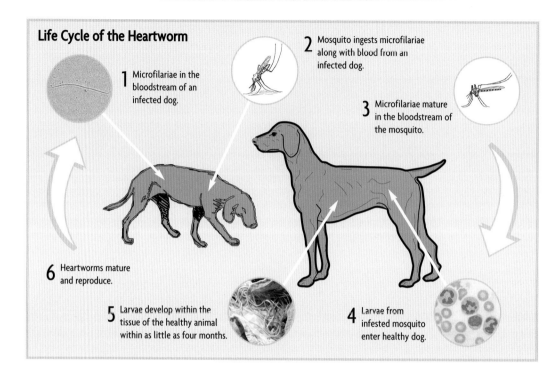

1 Microfilariae in the bloodstream of an infected dog.

2 Mosquito ingests microfilariae along with blood from an infected dog.

3 Microfilariae mature in the bloodstream of the mosquito.

4 Larvae from infested mosquito enter healthy dog.

5 Larvae develop within the tissue of the healthy animal within as little as four months.

6 Heartworms mature and reproduce.

HEARTWORMS

Heartworms are thin, extended worms up to 12 inches long, which live in a dog's heart and the major blood vessels surrounding it. Dogs may have up to 200 worms. Symptoms may be loss of energy, loss of appetite, coughing, the development of a pot belly and anemia.

Heartworms are transmitted by mosquitoes. The mosquito drinks the blood of an infected dog and takes in larvae with the blood. The larvae, called microfilariae, develop within the body of the mosquito and are passed on to the next dog bitten after the larvae mature. It takes two to three weeks for the larvae to develop to the infective stage within the body of the mosquito. Dogs are usually treated at about six weeks of age and maintained on a prophylactic dose given monthly.

Blood testing for heartworms is not necessarily indicative of how seriously your dog is infected. Although this is a dangerous disease, it is not easy for a dog to be infected. Discuss the various preventatives with your vet, as there are many different types now available. Together you can decide on a safe course of prevention for your dog.

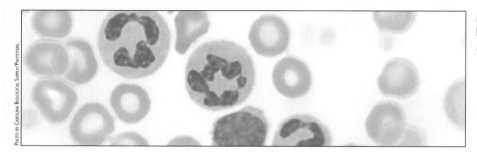

Magnified heartworm larvae, *Dirofilaria immitis*.

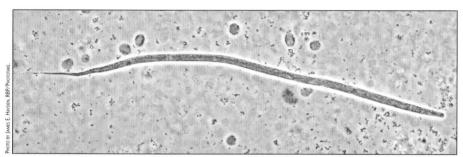

Heartworm, *Dirofilaria immitis*.

The heart of a dog infected with canine heartworm, *Dirofilaria immitis*.

HOMEOPATHY:
an alternative
to conventional
medicine

"Less is Most"

Using this principle, the strength of a homeopathic remedy is measured by the number of serial dilutions that were undertaken to create it. The greater the number of serial dilutions, the greater the strength of the homeopathic remedy. The potency of a remedy that has been made by making a dilution of 1 part in 100 parts (or 1/100) is 1c or 1cH. If this remedy is subjected to a series of further dilutions, each one being 1/100, a more dilute and stronger remedy is produced. If the remedy is diluted in this way six times, it is called 6c or 6cH. A dilution of 6c is 1 part in 1,000,000,000,000. In general, higher potencies in more frequent doses are better for acute symptoms and lower potencies in more infrequent doses are more useful for chronic, long-standing problems.

CURING OUR DOGS NATURALLY

Holistic medicine means treating the whole animal as a unique, perfect, living being. Generally, holistic treatments do not suppress the symptoms that the body naturally produces, as do most medications prescribed by conventional doctors and vets. Holistic methods seek to cure disease by regaining balance and harmony in the patient's environment. Some of these methods include use of nutritional therapy, herbs, flower essences, aromatherapy, acupuncture, massage, chiropractic and, of course, the most popular holistic approach, homeopathy.

Homeopathy is a theory or system of treating illness with small doses of substances which, if administered in larger quantities, would produce the symptoms that the patient already has. This approach is often described as "like cures like." Although modern veterinary medicine is geared toward the "quick fix," homeopathy relies on the belief that, given the time, the body is able to heal itself and return to its natural, healthy state.

Choosing a remedy to cure a problem in our dogs is the difficult part of homeopathy. Consult with your vet for a professional diagnosis of your dog's symptoms. Often these symptoms require

immediate conventional care. If your vet is willing and knowledgeable, you may attempt a homeopathic remedy. Be aware that cortisone prevents homeopathic remedies from working. There are hundreds of possibilities and combinations to cure many problems in dogs, from basic physical problems such as excessive shedding, fleas or other parasites, unattractive doggy odor, bad breath, upset tummy, obesity, dry, oily or dull coat, diarrhea, ear problems or eye discharge (including tears and dry or mucousy matter), to behavioral abnormalities such as fear of loud noises, habitual licking, poor appetite, excessive barking and various phobias. From alumina to zincum metallicum, the remedies span the planet and the imagination…from flowers and weeds to chemicals, insect droppings, diesel smoke and volcanic ash.

Using "Like to Treat Like"

Unlike conventional medicines that suppress symptoms, homeopathic remedies treat illnesses with small doses of substances that, if administered in larger quantities, would produce the symptoms that the patient already has. While the same homeopathic remedy can be used to treat different symptoms in different dogs, here are some interesting remedies and their uses.

Apis Mellifica
(made from honey bee venom) can be used for allergies or to reduce swelling that occurs in acutely infected kidneys.

Diesel Smoke
can be used to help control travel sickness.

Calcarea Fluorica
(made from calcium fluoride, which helps harden bone structure) can be useful in treating hard lumps in tissues.

Natrum Muriaticum
(made from common salt, sodium chloride) is useful in treating thin, thirsty dogs.

Nitricum Acidum
(made from nitric acid) is used for symptoms you would expect to see from contact with acids, such as lesions, especially where the skin joins the linings of body orifices or openings such as the lips and nostrils.

Symphytum
(made from the herb Knitbone, *Symphytum officianale*) is used to encourage bones to heal.

Urtica Urens
(made from the common stinging nettle) is used in treating painful, irritating rashes.

HOMEOPATHIC REMEDIES FOR YOUR DOG

Symptom/Ailment	Possible Remedy
ALLERGIES	Apis Mellifica 30c, Astacus Fluviatilis 6c, Pulsatilla 30c, Urtica Urens 6c
ALOPECIA	Alumina 30c, Lycopodium 30c, Sepia 30c, Thallium 6c
ANAL GLANDS (BLOCKED)	Hepar Sulphuris Calcareum 30c, Sanicula 6c, Silicea 6c
ARTHRITIS	Rhus Toxicodendron 6c, Bryonia Alba 6c
CANINE COUGH	Drosera 6c, Ipecacuanha 30c
CATARACT	Calcarea Carbonica 6c, Conium Maculatum 6c, Phosphorus 30c, Silicea 30c
CONSTIPATION	Alumina 6c, Carbo Vegetabilis 30c, Graphites 6c, Nitricum Acidum 30c, Silicea 6c
COUGHING	Aconitum Napellus 6c, Belladonna 30c, Hyoscyamus Niger 30c, Phosphorus 30c
DIARRHEA	Arsenicum Album 30c, Aconitum Napellus 6c, Chamomilla 30c, Mercurius Corrosivus 30c
DRY EYE	Zincum Metallicum 30c
EAR PROBLEMS	Aconitum Napellus 30c, Belladonna 30c, Hepar Sulphuris 30c, Tellurium 30c, Psorinum 200c
EYE PROBLEMS	Borax 6c, Aconitum Napellus 30c, Graphites 6c, Staphysagria 6c, Thuja Occidentalis 30c
GLAUCOMA	Aconitum Napellus 30c, Apis Mellifica 6c, Phosphorus 30c
HEAT STROKE	Belladonna 30c, Gelsemium Sempervirens 30c, Sulphur 30c
HICCOUGHS	Cinchona Deficinalis 6c
HIP DYSPLASIA	Colocynthis 6c, Rhus Toxicodendron 6c, Bryonia Alba 6c
INCONTINENCE	Argentum Nitricum 6c, Causticum 30c, Conium Maculatum 30c, Pulsatilla 30c, Sepia 30c
INSECT BITES	Apis Mellifica 30c, Cantharis 30c, Hypericum Perforatum 6c, Urtica Urens 30c
ITCHING	Alumina 30c, Arsenicum Album 30c, Carbo Vegetabilis 30c, Hypericum Perforatum 6c, Mezerium 6c, Sulphur 30c
MASTITIS	Apis Mellifica 30c, Belladonna 30c, Urtica Urens 1m
MOTION SICKNESS	Cocculus 6c, Petroleum 6c
PATELLAR LUXATION	Gelsemium Sempervirens 6c, Rhus Toxicodendron 6c
PENIS PROBLEMS	Aconitum Napellus 30c, Hepar Sulphuris Calcareum 30c, Pulsatilla 30c, Thuja Occidentalis 6c
PUPPY TEETHING	Calcarea Carbonica 6c, Chamomilla 6c, Phytolacca 6c

Recognizing a Sick Dog

Unlike colicky babies and cranky children, our canine kids cannot tell us when they are feeling ill. Therefore, there are a number of signs that owners can identify to know that their dogs are not feeling well.

Take note for physical manifestations such as:

- unusual, bad odor, including bad breath
- excessive shedding
- wax in the ears, chronic ear irritation
- oily, flaky, dull haircoat
- mucus, tearing or similar discharge in the eyes
- fleas or mites
- mucus in stool, diarrhea
- sensitivity to petting or handling
- licking at paws, scratching face, etc.

Keep an eye out for behavioral changes as well, including:

- lethargy, idleness
- lack of patience or general irritability
- lack of interest in food
- phobias (fear of people, loud noises, etc.)
- strange behavior, suspicion, fear
- coprophagia
- more frequent barking
- whimpering, crying

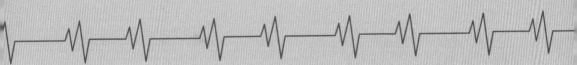

Get Well Soon

You don't need a DVM to provide good TLC to your sick or recovering dog, but you do need to pay attention to some details that normally wouldn't bother him. The following tips will aid Fido's recovery and get him back on his paws again:

- Keep his space free of irritating smells, like heavy perfumes and air fresheners.
- Rest is the best medicine! Avoid harsh lighting that will prevent your dog from sleeping. Shade him from bright sunlight during the day and dim the lights in the evening.
- Keep the noise level down. Animals are more sensitive to sound when they are sick.

- Be attentive to any necessary temperature adjustments. A dog with a fever needs a cool room and cold liquids. A bitch that is whelping or recovering from surgery will be more comfortable in a warm room, consuming warm liquids and food.
- You wouldn't send a sick child back to school early, so don't rush your dog back into a full routine until he seems absolutely ready.

Number-One Killer Disease in Dogs: CANCER

In every age, there is a word associated with a disease or plague that causes humans to shudder. In the 21st century, that word is "cancer." Just as cancer is the leading cause of death in humans, it claims nearly half the lives of dogs that die from a natural disease as well as half the dogs that die over the age of ten years.

Described as a genetic disease, cancer becomes a greater risk as the dog ages. Vets and dog owners have become increasingly aware of the threat of cancer to dogs. Statistics reveal that one dog in every five will develop cancer, the most common of which is skin cancer. Many cancers, including prostate, ovarian and breast cancer, can be avoided by spaying and neutering our dogs by the age of six months.

Early detection of cancer can save or extend a dog's life, so it is absolutely vital for owners to have their dogs examined by a qualified vet or oncologist immediately upon detection of any abnormality. Certain dietary guidelines have also proven to reduce the onset and spread of cancer. Foods based on fish rather than beef, due to the presence of Omega-3 fatty acids, are recommended. Other amino acids such as glutamine have significant benefits for canines, particularly those breeds that show a greater susceptibility to cancer.

Cancer management and treatments promise hope for future generations of canines. Since the disease is genetic, breeders should never breed a dog whose parents, grandparents and any related siblings have developed cancer. It is difficult to know whether to exclude an otherwise healthy dog from a breeding program, as the disease does not manifest itself until the dog's senior years.

RECOGNIZE CANCER WARNING SIGNS

Since early detection can possibly rescue your dog from becoming a cancer statistic, it is essential for owners to recognize the possible signs and seek the assistance of a qualified professional.

- Abnormal bumps or lumps that continue to grow
- Bleeding or discharge from any body cavity
- Persistent stiffness or lameness
- Recurrent sores or sores that do not heal
- Inappetence
- Breathing difficulties
- Weight loss
- Bad breath or odors
- General malaise and fatigue
- Eating and swallowing problems
- Difficulty urinating and defecating

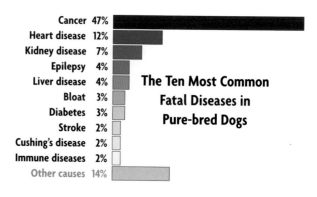

Cancer	47%
Heart disease	12%
Kidney disease	7%
Epilepsy	4%
Liver disease	4%
Bloat	3%
Diabetes	3%
Stroke	2%
Cushing's disease	2%
Immune diseases	2%
Other causes	14%

The Ten Most Common Fatal Diseases in Pure-bred Dogs

CDS: COGNITIVE DYSFUNCTION SYNDROME
"Old-Dog Syndrome"

There are many ways for you to evaluate old-dog syndrome. Veterinarians have defined CDS (cognitive dysfunction syndrome) as the gradual deterioration of cognitive abilities. These are indicated by changes in the dog's behavior. When a dog changes his routine response, and maladies have been eliminated as the cause of these behavioral changes, then CDS is the usual diagnosis.

More than half the dogs over eight years old suffer from some form of CDS. The older the dog, the more chance he has of suffering from CDS. In humans, doctors often dismiss the CDS behavioral changes as part of "winding down."

There are four major signs of CDS: frequent potty accidents inside the home, sleeping much more or much less than normal, acting confused and failing to respond to social stimuli.

SYMPTOMS OF CDS

FREQUENT POTTY ACCIDENTS
- *Urinates in the house.*
- *Defecates in the house.*
- *Doesn't signal that he wants to go out.*

SLEEP PATTERNS
- *Awakens more slowly.*
- *Sleeps more than normal during the day.*
- *Sleeps less during the night.*

CONFUSION
- *Goes outside and just stands there.*
- *Appears confused with a faraway look in his eyes.*
- *Hides more often.*
- *Doesn't recognize friends.*
- *Doesn't come when called.*
- *Walks around listlessly and without a destination.*

FAILURE TO RESPOND TO SOCIAL STIMULI
- *Comes to people less frequently, whether called or not.*
- *Doesn't tolerate petting for more than a short time.*
- *Doesn't come to the door when you return home.*

JAPANESE SPITZ

The term *old* is a qualitative term. For dogs, as well as for their masters, old is relative. Certainly we can all distinguish between a puppy Japanese Spitz and an adult Japanese Spitz—there are the obvious physical traits, such as size, appearance and facial expressions, and personality traits as well. Puppies and young dogs like to play with children. Children's natural exuberance is a good match for the seemingly endless energy of young dogs. They like to run, jump, chase and retrieve. When dogs grow older and cease their interaction with children, they are often thought of as being too old to keep pace with the children. On the other hand, if a Japanese Spitz is only exposed to people with quieter lifestyles, his life will normally be less active and the decrease in his activity level as he ages will not be as obvious.

If people live to be 100 years old, dogs live to be 20 years old. While this might sound like a viable rule of thumb, it is *very* inaccurate. When trying to compare dog years to human years, you cannot make a generalization about all dogs. Fortunately for Japanese Spitz

owners, the breed enjoys a long life, often to 14 years, sometimes 16 years or more.

Most dogs are considered physically mature at three years of age, although the early-blooming Japanese Spitz is fully mature by one year of age. Generally speaking, however, the first three years of a dog's life are like seven times that of comparable humans. That means a 3-year-old dog is like a 21-year-old human; with the Japanese Spitz, the 1-year-old is like an 18-year-old human! Thus, there is no hard and fast rule for comparing dog and human ages.

WHAT TO LOOK FOR IN SENIORS

Most breeders use the ten-year mark to consider the Japanese Spitz as a *senior*. This term does not imply that the dog is geriatric and has begun to fail in mind and body. Aging is essentially a slowing process. Humans readily admit that they feel a difference in their activity level from age 20 to 30, and then from 30 to 40, etc. By treating the ten-year-old dog as a senior, owners are able to implement certain therapeutic and preventative medical strategies with the help of their vets.

A senior-care program should include at least two veterinary visits per year and screening sessions to determine the dog's health status, as well as nutritional counseling. Veterinarians determine the senior dog's health status through a blood smear for a complete blood count, serum chemistry profile with electrolytes, urinalysis, blood pressure check, electrocardiogram, ocular tonometry (pressure on the eyeball) and dental prophylaxis.

Such an extensive program for senior dogs is well advised before owners start to see the obvious physical signs of aging, such as slower and inhibited movement, increased sleep/nap periods and disinterest in play and other activity. This preventative program promises a longer, healthier life for the aging dog. Among the physical problems common in aging dogs are the loss of sight and hearing, arthritis, kidney and liver failure, diabetes mellitus, heart disease and Cushing's disease (a hormonal disease).

In addition to the physical manifestations discussed, there are some behavioral changes and problems related to aging dogs. Dogs suffering from hearing or vision loss, dental discomfort or arthritis can become aggressive. Likewise, the near-deaf and/or

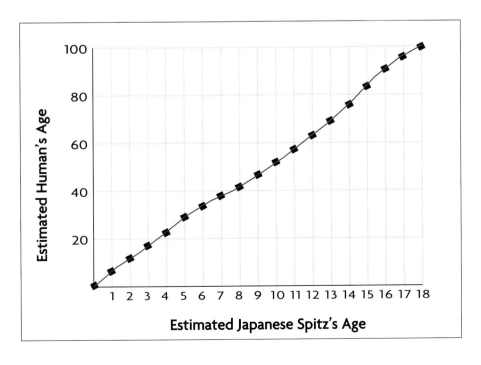

A Japanese Spitz youngster relaxes with an older friend, an ex-racing Greyhound who is showing the telltale graying on the muzzle and face.

blind dog may be startled more easily and react in an unexpectedly aggressive manner. Seniors suffering from senility can become more impatient and irritable. Housesoiling accidents are associated with loss of mobility, kidney problems and loss of sphincter control as well as plaque accumulation, physiological brain changes and reactions to medications. Older dogs, just like young puppies, suffer from separation anxiety, which can lead to excessive barking, whining, housesoiling and destructive behavior. Seniors may become fearful of everyday sounds, such as vacuum cleaners, heaters, thunder and passing traffic. Some dogs have difficulty sleeping, due to discomfort, the need for frequent toilet visits and the like.

Owners should avoid spoiling the older dog with too many treats. Obesity is a common problem in older dogs and subtracts years from their lives. Keep the senior dog as trim as possible, since excess weight puts

CONSISTENCY COUNTS

Puppies and older dogs are very similar in their need for consistency in their lives. Older pets may experience hearing and vision loss, or may just be more easily confused by changes in their homes. Try to keep things consistent for the senior dog. For example, doors that are always open or closed should remain so. Most importantly, don't dismiss a pet just because he's getting old; most senior dogs remain active and important parts of their owners' lives.

additional stress on the body's vital organs. Some breeders recommend supplementing the diet with foods high in fiber and lower in calories. Adding fresh vegetables and marrow broth to the senior's diet makes a tasty, low-calorie, low-fat supplement.

Your dog, as he nears his twilight years, needs your patience and good care more than ever. Never punish an older dog for an accident or abnormal behavior. For all the years of love, protection and companionship that your dog has provided, he deserves special attention and courtesies. The older dog may need to relieve himself at 3 a.m. because he can no longer hold it for eight hours. Older dogs may not be able to remain crated for more than two or three hours. It may be time to give up a sofa or chair to your old friend. Although

The second time around! This older Japanese Spitz was adopted later in life and found himself a wonderful home.

he may not seem as enthusiastic about your attention and petting, he does appreciate the considerations you offer as he gets older.

Your Japanese Spitz does not understand why his world is slowing down. Owners must make their dogs' transition into their golden years as pleasant and rewarding as possible.

WHAT TO DO WHEN THE TIME COMES

You are never fully prepared to make a rational decision about putting your dog to sleep. It is very obvious that you love your Japanese Spitz or you would not be reading this book. Putting a beloved dog to sleep is extremely difficult. It is a decision that must

---

HORMONAL PROBLEMS

Although graying is normal and expected in older dogs, a flaky coat or loss of hair is not. Such coat problems may point to a hormonal problem. Hypothyroidism, in which the thyroid gland fails to produce the normal amount of hormones, is one such problem. Your veterinarian can treat hypothyroidism with an oral supplement. The condition is more common in certain breeds, so discuss its likelihood in your Japanese Spitz with your breeder and vet.

EUTHANASIA SERVICES

Euthanasia must be done by a licensed vet, who may be considerate enough to come to your home. There also may be societies for the prevention of cruelty to animals in your area. They often offer this service upon a veterinarian's recommendation.

be made with your veterinarian. You are usually forced to make the decision when your dog experiences one or more life-threatening symptoms, requiring you to seek veterinary assistance. If the prognosis of the malady indicates that the end is near and that your beloved pet will only continue to suffer and experience no enjoyment for the balance of his life, then euthanasia is the right choice.

WHAT IS EUTHANASIA?

Euthanasia derives from the Greek, meaning *good death*. In other words, it is the planned, painless killing of a dog suffering from a painful, incurable condition, or who is so aged that he cannot walk, see, eat or control his excretory functions. Euthanasia is usually accomplished by injection with an overdose of anesthesia or a barbiturate. Aside from the prick of the needle, the experience is usually painless.

MAKING THE DECISION

The decision to euthanize your dog is never easy. The days during which the dog becomes ill and the end occurs can be unusually stressful for you. If this is your first experience with the death of a loved one, you may need the comfort dictated by your religious beliefs. If you are the head of the family and have children, you should have involved them in the decision of putting your Japanese Spitz to sleep. Usually your dog can be maintained on drugs at the vet's clinic for a few days in order to give you ample time to make a decision. During this time, talking with members of your family, clergy or people who have lived through the same experience can ease the burden of your inevitable decision.

THE FINAL RESTING PLACE

Dogs can have some of the same privileges as humans. The remains of your beloved dog can be buried in a pet cemetery, which is generally expensive. Alternatively, if your dog has died at home, he can be buried in your yard in a spot marked with a stone, flowers or a newly planted tree or shrub. Cremation is also an option; your dog can be cremated individually and the ashes returned to you. A less expensive option is mass cremation, although, of course, the ashes of individual dogs cannot then be returned.

Your vet will likely be able to recommend a pet cemetery in your locality if you choose to memorialize your beloved dog in this way.

Vets can usually help you locate a pet cemetery or arrange the cremation on your behalf. The cost of these options should always be discussed frankly and openly with your vet.

GETTING ANOTHER DOG?

The grief of losing your beloved dog will be as lasting as the grief of losing a human friend or relative. In most cases, if your dog died of old age (if there is such a thing), he had slowed down considerably. Do you now want a new Japanese Spitz puppy? Or are you better off adopting or rescuing a more mature Japanese Spitz, which will usually be housebroken and will have an already-developed

personality. In this case, you can find out if you like each other after a few hours of being together, and you could be giving a second chance to a wonderful dog.

The decision is, of course, your own. Do you want another Japanese Spitz or perhaps a different breed so as to avoid comparison with your beloved friend? Most people usually stay with the same breed because they know and love the characteristics of that breed. Then, too, they often know people who have the same breed and perhaps they are lucky enough that a breeder whom they know and respect expects a litter soon. What could be better?

JAPANESE SPITZ

When you purchase your Japanese Spitz, you will make it clear to the breeder whether you want one just as a lovable companion and pet, or if you hope to be buying a Japanese Spitz with show prospects. No reputable breeder will sell you a young puppy and tell you that it is *definitely* of show quality, for so much can go wrong during the early months of a puppy's development. If you plan to show, what you will hopefully have acquired is a puppy with "show potential."

To the novice, exhibiting a Japanese Spitz in the show ring may look easy, but it takes a lot of hard work and devotion to do top winning at a show such as Crufts, the World Dog Show or ARBA's Cherry Blossom show, not to mention a little luck too!

CONFORMATION-SHOW BASICS

The first concept that the canine novice learns when watching a dog show is that each dog first competes against members of his own breed. Once the judge has selected the best member of each breed (Best of Breed), provided that the show is judged on a Group system, that chosen dog will compete with other dogs in his group. Finally, the dogs chosen first in each group will compete for Best in Show.

The second concept that you must understand is that the dogs are not actually compared against one another. The judge compares each dog against his breed standard, the written description of the ideal specimen that is approved by the hosting kennel club. While some early breed standards were indeed based on specific dogs that were famous or popular, many dedicated enthusiasts say that a perfect specimen, as described in the standard, has never walked into a show ring, has never been bred and, to the woe of dog breeders around the globe, does not exist. Breeders attempt to get as close to this ideal as possible with every litter, but theoretically the "perfect" dog is so elusive that it is impossible. (And if the "perfect" dog were born, breeders and judges would never agree that the dog was indeed "perfect.")

If you are interested in exploring the world of dog

showing, your best bet is to join your local breed club or the national parent club. In England, the breed club is called the Japanese Spitz Club. Breed clubs often host both regional and national specialties, shows only for Japanese Spitzen, which can include conformation as well as obedience and agility trials. Even if you have no intention of competing with your Japanese Spitz, a specialty is like a festival for lovers of the breed who congregate to share their favorite topic: the Japanese Spitz! Clubs also send out newsletters, and some organize training days and seminars in order that people may learn more about their chosen breed.

If your Japanese Spitz is six months of age or older and registered with a kennel club, you can enter him in the club's shows where the breed is offered classes. Provided that your Japanese Spitz does not have a disqualifying fault, he can compete. Only unaltered dogs can be entered in a dog show, so if you have spayed or neutered your Japanese Spitz, your dog cannot compete in conformation. The reason for this is simple. Dog shows are the main forum to prove which representatives of a breed are worthy of being bred. Only dogs that have achieved championships—the dog world's "seal of approval" for excellence

CLUB CONTACTS

You can get information about dog shows from the national kennel clubs:

Fédération Cynologique Internationale
14, rue Leopold II, B-6530 Thuin, Belgium
www.fci.be

The Kennel Club
1-5 Clarges St., Piccadilly, London
W1Y 8AB, UK
www.the-kennel-club.org.uk

American Rare Breed Association
9921 Frank Tippett Road
Cheltenham, MD 20623 USA
www.arba.org

in pure-bred dogs—should be bred. Altered dogs, however, can participate in other events such as obedience and agility trials.

Before you actually step into the ring, you would be well advised to sit back and observe the judge's ring procedure. If it is your first time in the ring, do not be over-anxious and run to the front of the line. It is much better to stand back and study how the exhibitor in front of you is

do not be discouraged. Be patient and consistent, and you may eventually find yourself in a winning line-up. Remember that the winners were once in your shoes and have devoted many hours and much money to earn the placement. If you find that your dog is losing every time and never getting a nod, it may be time to consider a different dog sport or to just enjoy your Japanese Spitz as a pet. Parent clubs offer other events, such as agility, tracking, obedience, instinct tests and more, which may be of interest to the owner of a well-trained Japanese Spitz.

Shows are busy events in and out of the ring, equally enjoyed by participants and spectators.

performing. The judge asks each handler to "stack" the dog, hopefully showing the dog off to his best advantage. The judge will observe the dog from a distance and from different angles, and approach the dog to check his teeth, overall structure, alertness and muscle tone, as well as consider how well the dog "conforms" to the standard. Just as important, the judge will have the exhibitor move the dog around the ring in some pattern that he should specify. Finally, the judge will give the dog one last look before moving on to the next exhibitor.

If you are not in the top four in your class at your first show,

OBEDIENCE TRIALS
Obedience trials in the US trace back to the early 1930s when organized obedience training was developed to demonstrate how well dog and owner could work together. The pioneer of obedience trials is Mrs. Helen Whitehouse Walker, a Standard Poodle fancier, who designed a series of exercises after the Associated Sheep, Police, Army Dog Society of Great Britain. Since the days of Mrs. Walker, obedience trials have grown by leaps and bounds, and today there are thousands of trials held every year. Any registered dog can enter an obedience trial, regardless of conformational disqualifications or neutering.

FCI INFORMATION

There are 330 breeds recognized by the FCI, and each breed is considered to be "owned" by a specific country. Each breed standard is a cooperative effort between the breed's country and the FCI's Standards and Scientific Commissions. Judges use these official breed standards at shows held in FCI member countries. One of the functions of the FCI is to update and translate the breed standards into French, English, Spanish and German.

AGILITY TRIALS

The first organization to promote agility trials in the US was the United States Dog Agility Association, Inc. (USDAA). Established in 1986, the USDAA sparked the formation of many member clubs around the country. To participate in USDAA trials, dogs must be at least 18 months of age. In agility competition, the handler directs his dog through, over, under and around an obstacle course that includes jumps, tires, the dog walk, weave poles, pipe tunnels, collapsed tunnels and more. While working his way through the course, the dog must keep one eye and ear on the handler and the rest of his body on the course. The handler runs along with the dog, giving verbal and hand signals to guide the dog through the course.

The USDAA offers the titles Agility Dog (AD), Advanced Agility Dog (AAD) and Master Agility Dog (MAD) to winning dogs. The organization and its many affiliates throughout the country sponsor many events and programs each year. Other organizations/kennel clubs may sponsor agility trials under their own rules, sometimes held in conjunction with breed specialty shows.

Agility trials are a great way to keep your dog active, and they will keep you running, too! You should join a local agility club to learn more about the sport, whether you choose to compete or just train for fun and exercise. Agility clubs offer

Even with everything that's going on around him, a dog will stay focused in the show ring if his attention is centered on his handler—and a tasty treat to hold his interest doesn't hurt!

sessions to introduce dogs to the various obstacles as well as training classes to prepare for competition. In no time, your dog will be climbing A-frames, crossing the dog walk and flying over hurdles, all with you right beside him. Your heart will leap every time your dog jumps through the hoop—and you'll be having just as much (if not more) fun!

FÉDÉRATION CYNOLOGIQUE INTERNATIONALE

Established in 1911, the Fédération Cynologique Internationale (FCI) represents the "world kennel club." This international body brings uniformity to the breeding, judging and showing of pure-bred dogs. Although the FCI originally included only five European nations: France, Germany, Austria, the Netherlands and Belgium (which remains its headquarters), the

organization today embraces nations on six continents and recognizes well over 300 breeds of pure-bred dog.

The FCI sponsors both national and international shows. The hosting country determines the judging system and breed standards are always based on the breed's country of origin. Dogs from every country can participate in these impressive canine spectacles, the largest of which is the World Dog Show, hosted in a different country each year.

There are three titles attainable through the FCI: the International Champion, which is the most prestigious; the International Beauty Champion, which is based on aptitude certificates in different countries; and the International Trial Champion, which is based on achievement in obedience trials in different countries. An FCI title requires a dog to win three CACs (*Certificats d'Aptitude au Championnat*) at regional or club shows under three different judges who are breed specialists. The title of International Champion is gained by winning four CACIBs (*Certificats d'Aptitude au Championnat International de Beauté*), which are offered only at international shows, with at least a one-year lapse between the first and fourth award.

In addition to the hands-on physical evaluation, the judge also appraises each dog's movement as he gaits in the ring individually and as a group.

A young handler, pleased to have won her first Challenge Certificate (the building blocks to a UK championship) on her Japanese Spitz.

The FCI breeds are divided into ten groups. At the World Dog Show, the following classes are offered for each breed: Puppy Class (6–9 months), Junior Class (9–18 months), Open Class (15 months or older) and Champion Class. A dog can be awarded a classification of Excellent, Very Good, Good, Sufficient and Not Sufficient. Puppies can be awarded classifications of Very Promising, Promising or Not Promising. Four placements are made in each class. After all classes are judged, a Best of Breed is selected. Other special groups and classes may also be shown. Each exhibitor showing a dog receives a written evaluation from the judge.

Besides the World Dog Show, the European Championship Show and other all-breed shows, you can exhibit your dog at specialty shows held by different breed clubs. Specialty shows may have their own regulations.

Small breeds, the Japanese Spitz included, are put up on a table to enable thorough examination by the show judge.

As a Japanese Spitz owner, you have selected your dog so that you and your loved ones can have a companion, a protector, a friend and a four-legged family member. You invest time, money and effort to care for and train the family's new charge. Of course, this chosen canine behaves perfectly! Well, perfectly like a *dog*.

THINK LIKE A DOG

Dogs do not think like humans, nor do humans think like dogs, though we try. Unfortunately, a dog is incapable of comprehending how humans think, so the responsibility falls on the owner to adopt a viable canine mindset. Dogs cannot rationalize, and dogs exist in the present moment. Many a dog owner makes the mistake in training of thinking that he can reprimand his dog for something the dog did a while ago. Basically, you cannot even reprimand a dog for something he did 20 seconds ago! Either catch him in the act or forget it! It is a waste of your and your dog's time—in his mind, you are reprimanding him for

whatever he is doing at that moment.

The following behavioral problems represent some which owners most commonly encounter. Every dog is unique and every situation is unique. No author could purport for you to solve your Japanese Spitz's problems simply by reading a chapter in a breed book. Here we outline some basic "dogspeak" so that owners' chances of solving behavioral problems are increased. Discuss bad habits with your vet and he can recommend a behavioral specialist to consult in appropriate cases. Since behavioral abnormalities are the main reason for owners' abandoning their pets, we hope that you will make a valiant effort to solve your Japanese Spitz's problems if they arise. Patience and understanding are virtues that must dwell in every pet-loving household.

SEPARATION ANXIETY

Recognized by behaviorists as the most common form of stress for dogs, separation anxiety can also lead to destructive behaviors in your dog. It's more than your Japanese Spitz's howling his displeasure at your leaving the house and his being left alone. This is a normal reaction, no different from the child who cries as his mother leaves him on the first day at school. Separation anxiety is more serious. In fact, if you are constantly with your dog, he will come to expect you with him all of the time, making it even more traumatic for him when you are not there.

Obviously, you enjoy spending time with your dog, and he thrives on your love and attention. However, it should not become a dependent relationship in which he is heartbroken without you. This broken heart can also bring on destructive behavior as well as loss of appetite, depression and lack of interest in play and interaction. Canine behaviorists have been spending much time and energy to help owners better understand the significance of this stressful condition.

One thing you can do to minimize separation anxiety is to make your entrances and exits as low-key as possible. Do not give your dog long drawn-out goodbyes, and do not lavish him with hugs and kisses when you return. This is giving in to the attention that he craves, and it will only make him miss it more

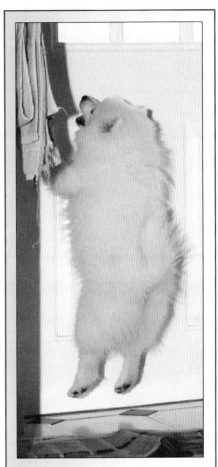

I'M HOME!
Dogs left alone for varying lengths of time may often react wildly when their owners return. Sometimes they run, jump, bite, chew, tear things apart, wet themselves, gobble their food or behave in very undisciplined ways. If your dog behaves in this manner upon your return home, allow him to calm down before greeting him or he will consider your attention as a reward for his antics.

when you are away. Another thing you can try is to give your dog a treat when you leave; this will not only keep him occupied and keep his mind off the fact that you have just left, but it will also help him associate your leaving with a pleasant experience.

You may have to accustom your dog to being left alone in intervals. Of course, when your dog starts whimpering as you approach the door, your first instinct will be to run to him and comfort him, but do not do it! Really—eventually he will adjust to your absence. His anxiety stems from being placed in an unfamiliar situation; by familiarizing him with being alone, he will learn that he will survive. That is not to say you should purposely leave your dog home alone, but the dog needs to know that, while he can depend on you

Your Japanese Spitz may like to curl up in out-of-the-way "dens" in the home, but he should not shy away or hide from contact with his people, as this indicates a fearful pup.

> ### NO BUTTS ABOUT IT!
> Dogs get to know each other by sniffing each other's backsides. It seems that each dog has a telltale odor, probably created by the anal glands. It also distinguishes sex and signals when a female will be receptive to a male's attention. Some dogs snap at another dog's intrusion of their private parts.

for his care, you do not have to be by his side 24 hours a day. Some behaviorists recommend tiring the dog out before you leave home—take him for a good long walk or engage in a game of fetch in the yard.

When the dog is alone in the house, he should be placed in his crate—another distinct advantage to crate-training your dog. The crate should be placed in his familiar happy family area, where he normally sleeps and already feels comfortable, thereby making him feel more at ease when he is alone. Be sure to give the dog a special chew toy to enjoy while he settles into his crate.

AGGRESSION
This is a problem that concerns all responsible dog owners, although Japanese Spitz owners rarely have problems with aggressive tendencies in their dogs. Aggression can be a very big problem in dogs in general, and,

when not controlled, always becomes dangerous. Fortunately, the Japanese Spitz is a gregarious, dog-loving dog, particularly enjoying the company of larger dogs.

An aggressive dog, no matter the size, may lunge at, bite or even attack a person or another dog. Aggressive behavior is not to be tolerated. It is more than just inappropriate behavior; it is painful for a family to watch their dog become unpredictable in his behavior to the point where they are afraid of him. While not all aggressive behavior is dangerous, things like growling, baring teeth, etc., can be frightening. It is important to ascertain why the dog is acting in this manner. Aggression is a display of dominance, and the dog should not have the dominant role in his pack, which is, in this case, your family.

It is important not to challenge an aggressive dog, as this could provoke an attack. Observe your Japanese Spitz's body language. Does he make direct eye contact and stare? Does he try to make himself as large as possible: ears pricked, chest out, tail erect? Height and size signify authority in a dog pack—being taller or "above" another dog literally means that he is "above" in social status. These body signals tell you that your Japanese Spitz thinks he is in charge, a

problem that needs to be addressed. An aggressive dog is unpredictable; you never know when he is going to strike and what he is going to do. You cannot understand why a dog that is playful one minute is growling the next.

Fear is a common cause of aggression in dogs. Perhaps your Japanese Spitz had a negative experience as a puppy, which causes him to be fearful when a similar situation presents itself later in life. The dog may act aggressively in order to protect himself from whatever is making him afraid. It is not always easy to determine what is making your dog fearful, but if you can isolate what brings out the fear reaction, you can help the dog get over it.

Supervise your dog's interactions with people and other dogs, and praise the dog when it goes well. If he starts to act aggressively in a situation, correct him and remove him from the

---

IT'S PLAY TIME

Physical games like pulling contests, wrestling, jumping and teasing should not be encouraged. Inciting a dog's crazy behavior tends to confuse him. The owner has to be able to control his dog at all times. Even in play, your dog has to know that you are the leader and that you decide when to play and when to calm down.

The competition is on for the title of "top dog." Dogs establish pack position through games, roughhousing and other friendly posturing.

situation. Do not let people approach the dog and start petting him without your express permission. That way, you can have the dog sit to accept petting, and praise him when he behaves properly. You are focusing on praise and on modifying his behavior by rewarding him when he acts appropriately. By being gentle and by supervising his interactions, you are showing him that there is no need to be afraid or defensive.

The best solution is to consult a behavioral specialist, one who has experience with the Japanese Spitz or similar breeds if possible. Together, perhaps you can pinpoint the cause of your dog's aggression and do something about it. An aggressive dog cannot be trusted, and a dog that cannot be trusted is not safe to have as a family pet. If, very unusually, you find that your pet has become untrustworthy and you feel it necessary to seek a new home

with a more suitable family and environment, explain fully to the new owners all your reasons for rehoming the dog to be fair to all concerned.

SEXUAL BEHAVIOR
Dogs exhibit certain sexual behaviors that may have influenced your choice of male or female when you first purchased your Japanese Spitz. To a certain extent, spaying/neutering will eliminate these behaviors, but if you are purchasing a dog that you wish to breed from, you should be aware of what you will have to deal with throughout the dog's life.

Female dogs usually have two estruses per year, with each season lasting about three weeks. These are the only times in which a female dog will mate, and she usually will not allow this until the second week of the cycle, although this varies from bitch to bitch. If not bred during the heat cycle, it is not uncommon for a bitch to experience a false pregnancy, in which her mammary glands swell and she exhibits maternal tendencies toward toys or other objects.

With male dogs, owners must be aware that whole dogs (dogs who are not neutered) have the natural inclination to mark their territory. Males mark their territory by spraying small amounts of urine as they lift their legs in a macho ritual. Marking can occur both outdoors in the yard and around the neighborhood as well as indoors on furniture legs, curtains and the sofa. Such behavior can be very frustrating for the owner; early training is strongly urged before the "urge" strikes your dog. Neutering the male at an appropriate early age can solve this problem before it becomes a habit.

Other problems associated with males are wandering and mounting. Both of these habits, of course, belong to the unneutered dog, whose sexual drive leads him away from home in search of the bitch in heat. Males will mount females in heat, as well as any other dog, male or female, that happens to catch their fancy. Other possible mounting partners include his owner, the furniture, guests to the home and strangers on the street. Discourage such behavior early on.

Owners must further recognize that mounting is not merely a sexual expression but also one of dominance, seen in males and females alike. Be consistent and be persistent, and you will find that you can "move mounters."

CHEWING

The national canine pastime is chewing! Every dog loves to sink his "canines" into a tasty bone, so

"X" MARKS THE SPOT

As a pack animal, your dog marks his territory as a way of letting any possible intruders know that this is his space and that he will defend his territory if necessary. Your dog marks by urinating because urine contains pheromones that allow other canines to identify him. While this behavior seems like a nuisance, it speaks volumes about your dog's mental health. Stable, well-trained dogs living in quiet, less populated areas may mark less frequently than less confident dogs inhabiting busy urban areas that attract many possible invaders. If your dog only marks in certain areas in your home, like your bed or the front door, these are the areas he feels obligated to defend. If your dog marks frequently, see your veterinarian or an animal behaviorist.

it is important to provide your dog with appropriate chew toys so that he doesn't destroy your possessions or make a habit of gnawing on your hands and fingers. Dogs need to chew to massage their gums, to make their new teeth feel better and to exercise their jaws. This is a natural behavior that is deeply embedded in all things canine. Our role as owners is not to stop the dog's chewing, but rather to redirect it to positive, chew-worthy objects. Be an informed owner and purchase proper chew toys, like strong nylon bones, that will not splinter. Be sure that the objects are safe and durable, since your dog's safety is at risk. Again, the owner is responsible for ensuring a dog-proof environment.

The best answer is prevention; that is, put your shoes, handbags and other "tasty" objects in their proper places (out of the reach of the growing canine mouth). Direct your puppy to his toys whenever you see him "tasting" the furniture legs or the leg of your trousers. Make a loud noise to attract the pup's attention and immediately escort him to his chew toy and engage him with the toy for at least four minutes, praising and encouraging him all the while. An array of safe, interesting chew toys will keep your dog's mind and teeth occupied, and distracted from chewing on things he shouldn't.

Some trainers recommend deterrents, such as hot pepper, a bitter spice or a product designed for this purpose, to discourage the dog from chewing unwanted objects. Test these products with your own dog to see which works best before investing in large quantities.

JUMPING UP
Jumping up is a dog's friendly way of saying hello! Some dog owners do not mind when their dog jumps up. The problem arises when guests come to the house and the dog greets them in the same manner—whether they like it or not! However friendly the greeting may be, the chances are that your visitors will not appreciate your dog's enthusiasm. The dog will not be able to distinguish upon whom he can jump

Chewing is a natural canine behavior, and it is the owner's responsibility to direct his dog's chewing to safe items rather than things around the home and yard that could prove dangerous.

and whom he cannot. Therefore, it is probably best to discourage this behavior entirely.

Pick a command such as "Off" (avoid using "Down" since you will use that for the dog to lie down) and tell him "Off" when he jumps up. Place him on the ground on all fours and have him sit, praising him the whole time. Always lavish him with praise and petting when he is in the sit position. In this way, you can give him a warm affectionate greeting, let him know that you are as excited to see him as he is to see you and instill good manners at the same time!

DIGGING

Digging, which is seen as a destructive behavior to humans, is actually quite a natural behavior in dogs. Although terriers (the "earth dogs") are most closely associated with digging, some Japanese Spitzen have really found that they have the "paws" for the art of excavating. When digging occurs in your yard, it is actually a normal behavior redirected into something the dog can do in his everyday life. In the wild, a dog would be actively seeking food, making his own shelter, etc. He would be using his paws in a purposeful manner for his survival. Since you provide him with food and shelter, he has no need to use his paws for these purposes, and so the energy that

he would be using may manifest itself in the form of little holes all over your yard and flower beds.

Perhaps your dog is digging as a reaction to boredom—it is somewhat similar to someone eating a whole bag of chips in front of the TV—because they are there and there is nothing better to do! Basically, the answer is to provide the dog with adequate play and exercise so that his mind and paws are occupied, and so that he feels as if he is doing something useful.

Of course, digging is easiest to control if it is stopped as soon as possible, but it is often hard to catch a dog in the act. If your dog is a compulsive digger and is not easily distracted by other activities, you can designate an area on your property where he is allowed to dig. If you catch him digging in an off-limits area of the yard, immediately take him to the

Whether or not you allow your Japanese Spitz on the furniture is a matter of personal choice, but you must be consistent in enforcing the rules whatever you decide.

Not all barking and jumping up is bad; these are signals that your Japanese Spitz uses to communicate with you. In this case, the dog is trying to tell his owner that it's time to come inside.

approved area and praise him for digging there. Keep a close eye on him so that you can catch him in the act—that is the only way to make him understand what is permitted and what is not. If you take him to a hole he dug an hour ago and tell him "No," he will understand that you are not fond of holes, dirt or flowers. If you catch him while he is stifle-deep in your tulips, that is when he will get your message.

BARKING STANCE

Did you know that a dog is less likely to bark when sitting than standing? Watch your dog the next time that you suspect he is about to start barking. You'll notice that as he does, he gets up on all four feet. Hence, when teaching a dog to stop barking, it helps to get him to sit before you command him to be quiet.

BARKING

The "spitz" designation usually means that the dog has a lot to say! In the way of barking, however, Japanese Spitzen are quite discriminate in their vocal tendencies. This, of course, varies from dog to dog, so some Japanese Spitzen are less reticent than others.

Talkative dogs can be somewhat frustrating to owners, as it is not always easy to tell what a dog means by his bark—is he excited, happy, frightened or angry? Whatever it is that the dog is trying to say, he should not be punished for barking. It is only when the barking becomes excessive, and when the excessive barking becomes a bad habit, that the behavior needs to be modified.

Japanese Spitzen tend to use their barks purposefully to "sound the alarm." If an intruder came into your home in the middle of the night and your Japanese Spitz barked a warning, wouldn't you be pleased? You would probably

Show dogs must be well behaved amid the hustle and bustle of the show and its many people, dogs, noises and smells. The dogs usually spend at least part of their time in their crates as they await their turn in the ring.

deem your dog a hero, a wonderful guardian and protector of the home. On the other hand, if a friend drops by unexpectedly, rings the doorbell and is greeted with a sudden sharp bark, you would probably be annoyed at the dog. But in reality, isn't this just the same behavior? The dog does not know any better. Unless he sees who is at the door and it is someone he knows, he will bark as a means of vocalizing that his (and your) territory is being threatened. While your friend is not posing a threat, it is all the same to the dog. Barking is his means of letting you know that there is an intrusion, whether friend or foe, on your property. This type of barking is instinctive and should not be discouraged.

Excessive habitual barking, however, is a problem that should be corrected early on, and

Japanese Spitzen can become nuisance barkers if not properly trained from a young age. As your Japanese Spitz grows up, you will be able to tell when his barking is purposeful and when it is for no reason. You will become able to distinguish your dog's different barks and their meanings. For example, the bark when someone comes to the door will be different from the bark when he is excited to see you. It is similar to a person's tone of voice, except that the dog has to rely totally on tone of voice because he does not have the benefit of using words. An incessant barker will be evident at an early age.

There are some things that encourage a dog to bark. For example, if your dog barks non-stop for a few minutes and you give him a treat to quiet him, he believes that you are rewarding him for barking. He will associate barking with getting a treat and will keep doing it until he is rewarded. On the other hand, if you give him a command such as "Quiet" and praise him after he has stopped barking for a few seconds, he will get the idea that being "quiet" is what you want him to do.

FOOD STEALING
Is your dog devising ways of stealing food from your coffee table or kitchen counter? If so, you must answer the following

HE'S PROTECTING YOU

Barking is your dog's way of protecting you. If he barks at a stranger walking past your house, a moving car or a fleeing cat, he is merely exercising his responsibility to protect his pack (*you*) and territory from a perceived intruder. Since the "intruder" usually keeps going, the dog thinks his barking chased it away and he feels fulfilled. This behavior leads your overly vocal friend to believe that he is the "dog in charge."

questions: Is your Japanese Spitz a bit hungry, or is he "constantly famished" like many dogs seem to be? Face it, some dogs are more food-motivated than others. They are totally obsessed by the smell of food and can only think of their next meal. Food stealing is terrific fun and always yields a great reward—*food*, glorious food.

Your goal as an owner, therefore, is to be sensible about where food is placed in the home and to reprimand your dog whenever he is caught in the act of stealing. But remember, only reprimand your dog if you actually see him stealing, not later when the crime is discovered; that will be of no use at all and will only serve to confuse him.

BEGGING

Just like food stealing, begging is a favorite pastime of hungry puppies! It achieves that same fabulous result—*food*! Dogs quickly learn that their owners keep the "good food" for themselves, and that we humans do not dine on kibble alone. Begging is a conditioned response related to a specific stimulus, time and place. The sounds of the kitchen, cans and bottles opening, crinkling bags, the smell of food in preparation, etc., will excite the dog, and soon the paws will be in the air!

Here is the solution to stopping this behavior: Never give

in to a beggar! You are rewarding the dog for sitting pretty, jumping up, whining and rubbing his nose into you by giving him food. By ignoring the dog, you will (eventually) force the behavior into extinction. Note that the behavior is likely to get worse before it disappears, so be sure there are not any "softies" in the family who will give in to little "Oliver" every time he whimpers, "More, please."

As you see this Japanese Spitz dance on his hind legs at the sight of a treat, is there any doubt that dogs respond to food?

My Japanese Spitz

PUT YOUR PUPPY'S FIRST PICTURE HERE

Dog's Name _____

Date _____ Photographer _____